AF540862

EFFECTIVE SCHOOLING

By

Dr. Marlow Ediger
M.S. Education, Ph.D.
Professor Emeritus in Education
Truman State University
Box 417, 201 W, 22nd St
North Newton KS 67117
United States of America

&

Dr. Digumarti Bhaskara Rao
M.Sc., M.A., M.A., M.Ed., Ph.D.
Reader & Research Director
R.V.R. College of Education
Guntur – 522006, A.P.

DISCOVERY PUBLISHING HOUSE PVT. LTD.
NEW DELHI-110 002

First Published - 2010

Reprinted - 2016

ISBN: 978-81-8356-613-1

Effective Schooling

Published by:

DISCOVERY PUBLISHING HOUSE PVT. LTD.
4383/4B, Ansari Road, Darya Ganj
New Delhi-110 002 (India)
Phone: +91-11-23279245, 43596064-65
Fax: +91-11-23253475
E-mail: discoverypublishinghouse@gmail.com
sales@discoverypublishinggroup.com
web: www.discoverypublishinggroup.com

Printed at:
Infinity Imaging Systems
Delhi

Dedicated
to
PROF. MOHD. AKHTAR SIDDIQUI
Chairperson
National Council for Teacher Education
Government of India
New Delhi
in
recognition
of his
exceptional achievements
in the fields of
Education

Preface

The school is a temple of learning for the tender children. The infrastructure the equipment, the administrator, the teacher, the curriculum, the library, the laboratories, the academic atmosphere, the teacher-learning programmes, etc., play their legitimate role in making the school a successful one and the student a useful one.

This book is aimed at providing certain guidelines with regard to childhood, school climate, effective teaching, homework, discipline, leadership, tutoring, supervision, curriculum, values etc., in order to bring school effectiveness.

This book will be of great use to school curriculum designers and school teachers and school administrators.

Digumarti Bhaskara Rao

Sri Sai Soudha
D-43 S.V.N. Colony
Guntur - 522 006
(India)

CONTENTS

1

RESPECTING CHILDHOOD

There are a plethora of things which might well be done to respect childhood. At the present time, little is done to guarantee the welfare of young children. With approximately forty per cent of children living on or below the poverty level, it indicates that needs do exist. With a forty per cent figure of children receiving free or reduced price lunches in the public schools, much more must be done to meet food needs of children. What might be done to meet needs of children?

All children should have the right to nutritious diet every day. This necessary so that children can concentrate on learning and achieving mentally. There is much to learn and children start out being very curious about their natural and social environment. Having food needs met makes it so that a child may pay attention to additional learnings rather than dealing with feelings of hunger.

Adequate sleep and rest are also a necessity. Tired and overly tense children fail to achieve adequately. Thus, the home setting needs to be conducive to healthful living including sleep and rest in a clean, secure environment.

Clothing worn should be clean and suitable to the occasion. It needs to fit properly and be appropriate for the season at hand. Shabby, ill fitting clothing does not make for an adequate self-concept. Sometimes, pupils can be rude if a child's clothing is not conducive in making for a good physical appearance. There are agencies in society which are ready and willing to help with clothing needs of children (Fisher, 2006: 784-786).

A safe environment is also salient. Fearing abuse does not help the child to develop well socially. Living in a tough neighbourhood with drug sales and firing of arms makes for anxiety feelings about survival. Children do like to be loved and feel that they belong emotionally to a group in school and in society.

The school can do much to assist pupils in developing a feeling of belonging. The teacher must accept all children as having worth. He/she needs to work in the direction of all children in a class and school being accepting of others, regardless of socio-economic levels. Rude, aloof, and intimidating behaviours must be identified and modified. This takes time and effort by faculty, staff, administration, and pupils. But, it is indeed worthwhile to have as a major goal of the school being acceptance of all (Waldbart *et al.*, 2006).

The personal worth of each child must be emphasized in school. The curriculum must be adapted to where each pupil is presently in achievement. This is a starting point and from there on continuous progress needs to be stressed. Pressuring children to succeed is a negative procedure of teaching. A mediocre curriculum lacks challenge for learners. Thus, there is a point where each pupil may achieve with stimulating learning activities. Thus, pupils may show personal abilities and talents when learning activities are:

- meaningful and make sense
- interesting and appealing to the learner
- purposeful and possess reasons for achievement of objectives
- developmentally appropriate
- motivating and provide for individual differences
- respectful of pupils and are able to deal in a caring manner (Ediger and Rao, 2005).

Periodically, pupils should receive praise for work well done. Each person desires recognition for achieving well. All can receive praise when individual differences are adhered to in the instructional arena. Slow, average, and fast achievers being taught on their respective developmental levels, makes it so each may receive recognition for work well done (Ediger and Rao, 2006).

Educators have long sought to understand the dynamics of turning around low performing schools, but interest in the subject has clearly intensified, largely because of state and federal accountability initiatives and the prospect of serious consequences for schools that continue to exhibit low academic achievement.

National Educational Technology Standards (NETS) recommended the following pertaining to planning and designing learning environments and experiences:

- plan and design effective learning environments and experiences supported by technology
- design developmentally appropriate learning opportunities that apply technology—enhanced instructional strategies to support the diverse needs of students

- apply current research on teaching and learning with technology when planning learning environments and experiences
- identify and locate technology resources and evaluate them for accuracy and suitability
- plan for management of technology resources within the context of learning activities
- plan strategies to manage student learning in a technology enhanced environment (Social Education, 2006).

By caring children properly, we can educate them effectively.

REFERENCES

Duke, Daniel L. (2006), "What We Know and Don't Know About Improving Low- performing Schools". *Phi Delta Kappan,* 87 (10), 729-734.

Ediger, Marlow, and D. Bhaskara Rao (2005), *Quality School Education.* New Delhi, India: Discovery Publishing House.

Ediger, Marlow, and D. Bhaskara Rao (2006), *Issues in School Curriculum.* New Delhi, India: Discovery Publishing House.

Fisher, Douglas (2006), Keeping Adolescents "Alive and Kickin It", *Phi Delta Kappan,* 87 (10), 784-786.

National Council for the Social Studies, (2006), "Technology Position Statement and Guidelines", *Social Education,* 70 (5), 329-332.

Waldbart *et al.* (2006), "Invitation to Families in an Early Literacy Support Program", *The Reading Teacher,* 59 (8), 774-785.

Warschauer, Mark (2006), "Going One to One", *Educational Leadership,* 2006 (4), 34-38.

2

SCHOOL CLIMATE AND LEARNING

More attention needs to be focused upon school climate to facilitate learning. Too frequently, attention is given to establishing challenging academic objectives of instruction, largely or only. Having quality academic objectives for student achievement is important, but also salient is the atmosphere within which the objectives are to be attained. A learning environment needs to be in evidence which assists students to achieve well.

HARMONIOUS STUDENT RELATIONSHIPS

Developing well socially is important for students presently as well as in the future in society. When small group or committee endeavours are being emphasized in the classroom, there needs to be selected standards which need to prevail. Thus, participants need to respect each other. It is annoying to the participant when there are interruptions perating to what is being discussed. Too frequently, the ideas do not come out the way it was intended when a participant is interrupted. There are TV newscast models which reveal rude interruptions when a panel is responding to a news item. The same is true in a classroom when students fail to listen but want to talk only. Then too, there are selected learners who are ignored in a committee setting. For some reason, these shunned student's ideas are not considered as being worthwhile. A good rule to follow in small group work is that everyone has opportunities to participate actively. Ideas presented need to circulate among the participants (Ediger, 2005). Each person must speak clearly so that stated content is understandable. What is not clear needs to be restated so that meaningful learning accrues. A major problem in stressing an acceptable school climate is rude behaviour. Students and the teacher need to co-operatively develop rules of conduct which minimizes/eliminates rudeness as a form of behaviour. A student may not participate due to being ridiculed in the classroom or school setting. Rather, there needs to be encouragement for accepting each learner as a human being having much worth. Hosseini (2007) wrote:

> In co-operative learning, as a humanistic learner centered approach to education, intellectually selected heterogeneous teams of three to six members are motivated to work together on well designed learning tasks for the purpose of achieving their shared learning goals under conditions that meet the following criteria:
>
> (1) instructor as a fellow facilitator expert,
> (2) interaction soliciting tasks,
> (3) well designed grouping,
> (4) scheduled face to face interaction,
> (5) continuity of group interaction,
> (6) interpersonal and collaborative skills,

(7) positive interdependence,
(8) individual responsibility,
(9) equal participation,
(10) simultaneous interaction,
(11) reflection or group processing.

A learning exercise only qualifies as a modern Co-operative Learning to the extent that these pivotal features are present appropriately, if not equally (i.e., if, for example, individual accountability, in a Co-operative Learning situation, appears to be subordinated to positive interdependence, it cannot be considered a modern Co-operative Learning, albeit it may be deemed as group work). Thus, Co-operative Learning is more than a mere sitting together. It exists when students feel a need for co-operation and enthusiastically work together to attain their communal learning goals which they could never do otherwise.

Bullying is a major problem in many schools. This may occur in or outside the classroom. The bully might consist of one or more persons. The student due to physical appearance or dress, speaking with an accent or speaking slowly, among other characteristics, might well be subject to harassment. It is extremely uncomfortable to be the receiver and not positive for the doer of harassing. Negative feelings and attitudes result, especially of the one who is the target of harassment. Teachers in classrooms need to observe very carefully those who do the harassment which includes name calling, mimicking, hitting, tripping, and making others reputations "bad" through vicious gossip. Supervisors on playgrounds and in school hallways/lunchrooms must carefully monitor student actions. Politeness and acceptance of others is needed. Pertaining to the recent massacre of thirty two students at Virginia Tech University, the following writing was presented as a description of the one who did the murdering:

In high school, Cho Seung-Hui almost never opened his mouth.

When he finally did, his classmates laughed, pointed at him, and said, "Go back to China." . . . Cho was almost a textbook case of a school shooter; a painfully awkward, picked on young man who lashed out with methodical fury at a world he believed was out to get him.

When criminologists and psychologists look at mass murderers, Cho fits the themes they see repeatedly: a friendless figure, someone who has been bullied, someone who blames others and is bent on revenge, a careful planner, a male. . . . (*The Hutchinson News*, April 20, 2007). Bullying certainly needs to be avoided in all places and times.

Proper conduct and manners are necessary in the school lunchroom for breakfasts as well as lunch. For quality living to occur, students need to welcome others and to develop feelings of belonging. Each person desires to possess feelings of belonging. Within this framework, food and nutrition needs must be met for students to achieve as optimally as possible. Needy children should be given food to take home for the weekend. There is still a need for serving dinner, the evening meal, to students. Hopefully, this will be remedied and implemented, perhaps during break-time educational programs after the regular school day has been completed. No one can do well when being hungry. With considerable poverty in society, student lunch programs for the summer months also need to be implemented. Free transportation must be provided for those who have no way of getting to these centres.

SALIENT SKILLS TO DEVELOP

Thinking abilities need nurturing for students to make quality decisions within the framework of co-operative learning, as well as in society. Levine (2007), presents the following cognitive concepts for students to acquire in term of thinking skills:

- Forming, grasping, and applying concepts
- Accessing prior knowledge and experience
- Understanding through verbal, nonverbal, and experiential pathways
- Forming multiple vivid mental representations of new knowledge and ideas
- Monitoring degrees of comprehension
- Analyzing expectations (overt as well as unspoken)
- Actively processing information inputs
- Systematically evaluating ideas, issues, people, and products
- Assessing opportunities
- Actively processing information inputs
- Balancing of integrating detail with the "big picture"
- Finding a balance between "top down" and convergent thinking.

Students need to develop relevant thinking skills which will be useful presently as well as in the future societal arenas. The best choices and decisions must be made presently by students. Peer and societal pressures to use harmful drugs, alcohol, and engage in premarital sexual relations, among others, are harmful and require quality decision-making skills to avoid those things which ruin a person's chances at success in life. To assist in developing a good self-concept, the student needs to experience success in learning and receive recognition for achievement. Thus, meeting student *esteem* needs are important.

REFERENCES

Ediger, Marlow (2005), "Present Day Philosophies of Education", *Journal of Instructional Psychology*, 32 (3),179-182.

Hosseini, S. Mohammad Hassan (2007), "Aspects of Co-operative Learning", *Edutracks*, 6 (8) 7.

Levine, Mel (2007), "The Essential Cognitive Backpack", *Educational Leadership*, 64 (7), 19.

The Hutchinson, Kansas News (April 20, 2007), *Seung-Hui fit the mold of a school shooter*, pp 1, 2.

3

GOOD TEACHING AND LEARNING IN SCHOOLS

Teachers need to study diverse theories of teaching and learning in order to change, modify, and implement diverse strategies which may improve instructional procedures. Theories vary from each other by being highly structured as compared to those being more open ended. Styles of students in learning need to be considered when emphasizing a specific theory. Individual differences need adequate provision when stating objectives, learning opportunities, and assessment procedures. Each student needs to achieve as optimally as possible.

Behaviourism stresses the concept of precision in student learning. B.F. Skinner, a leading advocate, stressed the importance of reinforcement in learning. He advocated facts and skills to be identified for student learning. These are chosen prior to teaching and stated as objectives of instruction. Each objective is very precisely stated and not subject to interpretation as to its meaning. Each learning activity harmonizes with an objective. Thus, the activity is aligned with an objective. Either a student does/does not achieve an objective as a result of teaching.

Programmed learning strongly emphasizes behaviourism as a theory of learning. In a computerized program, the student responds to a brief selection of what was read on a monitor. Generally, the content to be read consists of a paragraph or less, depending upon the developmental level of the student. The learner responds to a test item, usually in multiple choice form, covering the subject matter read. He/she then checks the correctness of the response. If correct, the student is rewarded and the learning is then reinforced. If incorrect, the student sees the correct answer and is also ready for the next sequential item to be read. Read, respond, and check tends to be the sequence in learning, according to behaviourists in programmed learning. Correct responses are always to be reinforced. A computerized program might have a buzzer sound made for each correct response. The student, too, may notice on the monitor the per cent of answers given correctly. Facets of programmed learning may be stressed in the classroom when the teacher rewards correct responses with inexpensive prizes, praise, and free time given for students responding correctly in class.

Programmers write each computerized program for student interaction. They determine what is to be sequentially learned by the student as well as the correct responses to be made. These programs are generally field tested in pilot studies. In small steps, the student gradually moves forward toward increasingly more complex ideas. Ediger and Rao (2007), wrote the following pertaining to behaviourism as a psychology of learning and its contributions:

* It has made educators more cognizant about having precise objectives in teaching. Objectives certainly can be too broadly stated whereby they have little or no meaning in teaching, such as "To develop the democratic citizen".
* It has assisted educators in looking at objectives more thoroughly in terms of what is relevant. Why? High quality behaviourally stated objectives are time consuming to write, and therefore makes the writers conscious of the importance of what pupils are learning. If too many objectives need to be written, the chances are pupils are to learn trivial facts. Good behaviourally stated objectives are clearly written and state vital subject matter pupils are to learn.
* The evaluation process is simplified in that the student has/has not achieved the objective, as a result of instruction. The teacher can be relatively certain that the objectives have been achieved if written in a precise manner.

Somewhat toward the other end of the continuum is constructivism as a theory of learning. Here, the student has leeway in deciding upon what to learn, within a unit of study. Students, for example, may identify problems and questions in context. This is to be encouraged, and students may locate information from a variety of reference sources to find solutions to the identified problem areas. With teacher assistance as an encourager and motivator, students are guided to achieve on personal goals such as problem identification and solving. It is the student who develops and arrives at tentative truth, not dogma nor handed down answers.

Knowledge is tentative and subject to modification. Students tend to work in committees although individuals might also engage in problem solving activities. Constructionists believe that:

* knowledge and skills become more precise in ongoing experiences and is continuously refined
* learning by discovery is important and integrates what is done in school and in society
* the student is an active learner, not a passive recipient of content
* students become motivated learners when being actively engaged in learning and in constructing knowledge
* learners need to be involved in self-evaluation and in co-operative evaluation with teacher involvement.

Pertaining to a child centered school, Castleman and Littky (2007, p. 59), wrote the following:

> Decades ago, A.S. Neill sought to develop schools that would allow young people to flourish.

Neill writing in *Summerhill: A Radical Approach to Child Rearing* (1960), said:

> "We should allow young children to be themselves . . . my view is that a child is innately wise and realistic" (p. 4).

At Summerhill, students had the freedom and flexibility from an early age to explore what interested them. Neill esteemed student happiness as a primary educational goal and created a culture of love and approval that would encourage students to thrive.

Castleman and Littky (2007, p. 61), further emphasized the following in stressing a child centered school:

* Build structures which personalize leaning.
* Enable students to explore their interests in the real world.
* Find like-minded people in your school or community. Reach out to parents, community groups, and college students. Start a reading and discussion group.
* Attend a conference where you can meet like minded people from other areas. Big Picture, for example, hosts an annual conference that focuses on personalization.
* Start a school. Many communities, rural and urban, are looking for models that will engage students, make learning relevant and prepare students for life after high school.

Cognitive approaches in teaching and learning are somewhat in between behaviourism and constructivism. Cognitive psychology places much emphasis upon students possessing adequate background information before studying a new topic. Thus, to understand the objectives to be stressed in a new unit of study, students will need selected facts, concepts, and generalizations, as readiness factors for learning. The teacher needs to plan the order of readiness activities to assist students to attain each objective. Learners need to attend carefully to the subject matter content within each activity. Active engagement is necessary. It is important that students understand what is taught. Meaning theory is salient. Rote learning and memorization are opposites of meaningful experiences. However, review of what has been learned assists in retaining major ideas achieved. A variety of learning experiences are then necessary to assist learners in achieving, growing, and developing.

After students have experienced adequate readiness activities, they need to engage in a sequence of learnings which will assist in understanding increasingly complex ideas. Procedures used in teaching may include learning by discovery as well as deductively, teacher directed activities, textbook and internet use, as well as the utilization of a variety of reference sources. Individual differences need to be provided for. Obtaining student attention is vital in teaching and learning situations.

Meaningful outcomes of instruction are salient to determine for teaching/learning activities. Brown (2006), after studying for four consecutive summers a sample of what middle school teachers believed would prepare students for productive and successful lives prioritized the following objectives from respondents:

* Critical thinking skills
* Problem solving strategies and effective decision-making skills
* Creative thinking processes
* Effective oral and written communication skills
* Basic reading, mathematics, and writing abilities
* Knowledge of when and how to use research to solve problems
* Effective interpersonal skills
* Technology skills
* Knowledge of good health and hygiene skills
* Acceptance and understanding of diverse cultures and ethnicities

* Knowledge of how to effectively manage money
* Willingness, strategies, and ability to continue learning.

REFERENCES

Brown, Dave F. (2006), "It's the Curriculum Stupid: There's Something Wrong With It", *Phi Delta Kappan*, 87 (10), 778.

Castleman, Ben, and Dennis Littky (2007), "Learning to Love Learning", *Educational Leadership*, 64 (8), 59.

Ediger, Marlow, and D. Bhaskara Rao (2007), *Reading Curriculum and Instruction*. New Delhi, India: Discovery Publishing House, p. 74.

4

WHAT IS GOOD TEACHING IN SCHOOLS?

Good teaching needs to be defined carefully. A detailed study needs to be made to ascertain which ingredients make for excellence in education. A variety of reference sources need to be used, including print materials, audio-visual aids, as well as human resources. Ongoing revisions must be made as new ideas and research results accrue, resulting in possible revisions in teaching and learning situations. There is always room for improvement in educating students in any classroom or school system.

GOALS IN TEACHING

Staff development plans based on research findings and rational thought should be used as a foundation to improve instruction. The objectives for staff development should be clearly stated. Faculty members need to try out innovative ideas and report back to staff development members. Motivated teachers pursuing innovative ideas to up student achievement should be in the offing. Participants need to feel that purpose is involved in the staff development program. Without a communicated purpose, faculty will tend not to be enthusiastic about inservice education. There must be reasons for modifying teaching practices for staff development programs to be effective. Enthusiastic learning opportunities must prevail which encourage good teaching. High expectations must accrue for teachers to achieve optimally (Ediger and Rao, 2006).

Good teaching emphasizes that teachers assist students who have specific problems in learning for example, when diagnosing student difficulties in learning, assistance must be give to overcome the problem. This, if a student is not able to find the area of a circle, the student needs assistance in understanding the meaning of the symbol "pi (3.1417)", the meaning of "radius", and the meaning of "to square a number". The relationship in area between a square and a circle may be shown by transposing one of these geometrical figures over the other. Students establishing meaning in whatever is being learned is salient, presently, as well as for sequential learnings. If a student, then, is not able to solve a problem such as in mathematics, the teacher needs to assist students to understand the previous steps of meaning:

* understand the concepts of pi, radius, and squared
* develop the generalization for the finding the area of a circle: radius squared times pi (3. 1417)
* perform the needed operation in determining the area of a circle.

Teachers need to have ample time to work collaboratively with others be it in grade level meetings, team teaching, and/or in a workshop. In this way teachers face less isolation and learn from each other. Sharing ideas on good teaching is a must! Here, teachers may work on problems of their very own choosing. Individual differences/needs among teachers might well be provided for in these situations.

Decisions made pertaining to teaching may come from a variety of data sources including mandated test results, pupil daily products, teacher observation, diary entries from teachers written on learner achievement, and supervisor recorded statements on student progress. Decisions made should focus on the student and his/her needs in the school curriculum (Shepherd and Ragan, 1982).

Leadership provided by school administrators and supervisors must encourage innovative methods of teaching which are conducive to good teaching. School leaders must secure needed materials of instruction for teachers. They assist in securing not only vital materials of instruction for teaching and learning situations, but also assist teachers in using methods of instruction, conducive to aiding student achievement. Working together with a nearby university teacher education faculty, the local school becomes a beacon for improved instruction. High expectations from students need to be in the offing. Raising learner achievement through motivation, encouragement, and purposeful/interesting learning activities will help students presently in sequential achievement as well as at the future work place (Ediger and Rao, 2005).

The local school must have a professional library which contains recent journals in education on teaching each curriculum area. Teacher education textbooks should also be available for teacher perusal. Contents from professional reading may form the basis for discussion groups relegated to improving the curriculum. Special time needs to be set aside for faculty and administration discussing content read from professional reading.

Current technology might well assist students to achieve more optimally. All categories of students need to be helped such as English Language Learners (ELL), at risk students, special education pupils, as well as others in the school setting. Students need to achieve objectives of instruction and computer technology might well assist in this direction. The National Assessment of Educational Progress (NAESP) stated, in general, that technology does play a positive role in history when doing the following tasks more often:

* word processing. Students who are skillful at keyboarding can more easily express their ideas than students who scribble out their homework with pen and paper.
* Using computers for art projects. Although there may not be any history knowledge involved in creating computer graphics, this activity provides students with a set of conceptual tools that they can apply across subject areas.
* Creating charts, graphs, and tables. These tasks help students think abstractly about economics, social, and physical phenomenon.
* Using computers to complete school projects. Experience in planning, implementing, and sustaining a large project — a practice often referred to as "project - based learning"— appears to promote student achievement. An example is developing a Web site that incorporates knowledge from many different subject areas, such as a project on global warming that combines economics, physics, and data analysis.
* Using computers to communicate through e-mail and chat groups. This finding may surprise us; presumably students do not obtain an e-mail address

for the express purpose of completing their homework assignment. But if students have the e-mail address, it gives them the opportunity to discuss readings, homework assignments, and projects in various classes (Wenglinsky, 2006).

GOOD TEACHING

Good teaching is that which assists students to achieve valuable learnings. It provides for learners of all achievement levels and uses positive methods of instruction.

In creating an innovative school, districts must reshape their organizational structures and systems to spark the process of innovating and to sustain innovations. Five major actions are critical to making this happen:

* Adapt school designs that embody "edgy" innovations, operating at or beyond the boundaries of current practice. This is edge to-middle-change.
* Delve onto individual schools the creation of innovative programs and practices that substantially affect student learning and influence policy.
* Make innovations transparent to all, particularly the community.
* Create systematic innovations that integrate health, housing, and neighbourhood revitalizations.
* redesign system budget processes to accommodate the ways that small schools achieve economies of scale (Washor and Mojkowski, 2006).

REFERENCES

Ediger, Marlow, and D. Bhaskara Rao (2005), *Quality School Education*. New Delhi, India: Discovery Publishing House.

Ediger, Marlow, and D. Bhaskara Rao (2006), *Successful School Education*. New Delhi, India: Discovery Publishing House.

Shepherd, Gene, and William Ragan (1982), *Modern Elementary Curriculum*. New York: Holt, Rinehart and Winston.

Washor, Elliot, and Charles Mojkowski (2006), "Creating New Steps, Innovations from the Edge to the Middle", *Phi Delta Kappa*, 87 (10), 735-739.

Wenglinsky, Harold (2006), "Technology and Achievement, the Bottom Line", *Educational Leadership*, 63 (4), 29-32.

5

EFFECTIVE TEACHING IN SCHOOL CLASSROOM

There are Selected Methods of Instruction which need to be followed in order that students achieve well. They need to be followed and implemented flexibly to meet student needs. The needs of students change and do not remain static. By studying the learner and noticing the consequences of using recommended methods of instruction, the teacher realizes more fully what each student needs in order to attain more optimally.

THE STUDENT AND THE CURRICULUM

How does the teacher become one who teaches more effectively? The teacher needs to have a regular program of reading professional literature on teaching and learning. When comprehending its contents, the teacher needs to think of ways to effectively use in the classroom what has been read. Thus, the abstract is made concrete so that application of knowledge acquired is possible. Meaning attached to the abstract makes practical use of ideas learned. It is vital to experiment with new ideas, providing they are based on sound educational thinking.

In teaching students, illustrations help to make learnings more vivid when used at the proper time. Thus in reading ideas, the subject matter may not make sense until a picture is used for clarification purposes. Teachers need to have illustrations available when needed for teaching/learning situations. These refer to illustrations from power point slides, computer downloads, textbooks, and encyclopedias, among others. Understanding of what is read is vital (See Gulhane, 2006).

Sometimes movement is necessary to instill meaning such as the use of videos, CDs, and CD ROMS. In reading about the Middle Ages, observing a video on stages of becoming a knight or becoming a member of the guild is made vivid with motion of the participants. Judicious use of audio visual materials is necessary to avoid repetition, boredom, and sameness in teaching.

Suitable approaches of grouping for instruction is also important. The teacher needs to ascertain when large group, small group, and individual instruction is needed for more optimal learner achievement. Teaching the class as a whole may be ineffective at certain times due to individual differences and needs. Smaller groups may more likely assist those who need more help and attention. At other times, the individual needs specific assistance to achieve, develop, and grow. The major objective in grouping for instruction is to provide help to learners where it is most needed at different times (Ediger and Rao, 2006).

The teacher needs to be a good diagnostician to notice specific misconceptions that students may have. That is the point of intervention. Sequential learnings then need to be provided to overcome deficiencies. They may need to be scaffolded to achieve an objective. Meaning needs to be attached to ongoing experiences. Use and application must then be made of the new learning to reinforce understandings acquired. With many children in a classroom, the teacher needs to streamline operations so that each learner receives an appropriate education. Materials for instruction may need to be designed by the teacher to meet learner needs (See Liang and Dole, 2006).

A variety of methods need to be provided. These include inductive and deductive procedures as well as concrete, semi-concrete, and abstract activities. They need to be adapted to the present achievement level of students. No student should be allowed to fall through the cracks, but rather should be assisted to be as successful as possible. Continuous success on the part of each student is salient. It is important to have active participation of each learner in ongoing presentations. Passive students fail to achieve as much as their unique abilities permit.

Methods of teaching and learning should also be directly related to library use. Reading materials and audio-visual aids need to be readily available to assist learners to make continual progress. Library experiences should relate to ongoing lessons and units of study. Thus, library materials may relate to a topic being pursued in the classroom. This might well involve giving an oral or written book report, or a paper being developed. Students need to familiarize themselves with services offered by the school library. These services extend the learnings secured by students in the classroom. Then too, students should have ample opportunities to browse in the school library to develop interests in reading. New ideas might well accrue in wanting to check out books for home reading as well as reading during spare time in school. A positive attitude toward reading and school in general is desired (See Eisner, 2006).

What is learned by students should be shared during classroom discussions or in special sharing time which has been designated. Pictures and illustrations may be used by students during the sharing time. Rules during sharing should emphasize good listening, comprehension, curiosity, and asking questions. It is important for students to have quality human relations by being polite and being receptive to new ideas. Positive feelings and emotions go a long way in developing quality interactions among students (See Heuser, 2005).

Problem solving needs to be stressed in the school and classroom. There are problems to be solved for all. Throwing one's hands up in frustration and disgust is not an acceptable way to solve problems. Rather, each problem needs identification and solutions sought. The solutions may come from reading selected materials as well as from human resources.

Friendships need to be formed whereby there is trust among members. All desire to belong to a group of trusted friends, Feelings of belonging is a basic human need. A student who is an isolate has a great need to become a part of a reliable group. Acceptance and being caring in nature are viable traits for good human relationships. These traits make for a quality environment conducive to good mental hygiene.

Students need assistance in solving personal and social problems. Good human relations needs to extended to the entire faculty and staff within a school. Rudeness, aloofness, and hypocrisy are negatives and must be changed to an environment of trust, acceptance, and humaneness. Good human relations also aid in the development of intellectual capabilities. With respect toward others, higher levels of cognition may be stressed such as critical thinking. Critical thinking emphasizes analyzing information accrued in terms of being factual versus opinions, accurate from inaccurate statements, and/or being reliable versus unreliable information. Students feel freer to engage in critical thinking when the classroom environment is favourable. To think critically, the learner needs to feel free from restraints such as being ridiculed for the expressing of ideas. A good classroom environment also needs to be in evidence for creative thinking. Novel, unique ideas accrue from learners when there is an inner feeling to express originality of ideas. Thus, to brain storm involves playing with ideas. Ridiculing the thinking of others minimizes group participation in this activity. The more ideas received, the better when brain storming, such as the number of uses of a brick (See Bloodgood Pacifici, 2004).

Within any unit of academic study, it is salient for students to become proficient in critical and creative thinking. Life in society demands proficiency in thinking on the part of each person.

INSERVICE EDUCATION

Inservice education programs should assist teachers to move from what is to what should be. The old has passed away and all things are new, in part. Satisfactory parts of the older methods of instruction remain. Inservice education for teachers should emphasize:

- respecting and accepting each other in the school and classroom setting.
- emphasizing students engaging in higher levels of thinking and cognition.

- using a variety of teaching methods to provide for individual differences among students.

These, among others, need to be tried out in actual teaching and learning situations. Feedback to teachers in the workshop need to be informed of the successes and lack thereof in using new procedures of instruction. The school curriculum needs to change to aid learners to achieve more optimally.

The National Council for the Social Studies has issued a position statement on technological use in schools titled "Technology Position Statement and Guidelines" which include the following:

Teaching, Learning, and the Curriculum: Social Studies Educators:

- teachers implement curriculum plans that include methods and strategies for applying technology to maximize student learning in social studies;
- facilitate technology enhanced experiences that address content standards and student technology standards;
- use technology to support learner centered strategies that address the diverse needs of students;
- apply technology to develop student's higher order skills and creativity;
- manage student learning activities in a technology-enhanced environment.

Assessment and Evaluation: Social Studies Educators:

- apply technology through a variety of strategies to assess student learning in the social studies;
- apply technology in assessing student learning of

subject matter using a variety of assessment techniques

- use technology resources to collect and analyze data, interpret results, and communicate findings to improve instructional practice and maximize student learning;
- apply multiple methods of evaluation determine students' appropriate use of technology resources (Social Education, 2006).

Technology needs to be incorporated into the curriculum to assist students to achieve as optimally as possible.

REFERENCES

Bloodgood, Janet W., Linda C. Pacifici (2004), "Bringing Word Study to Intermediate Classrooms", *The Reading Teacher*, 58 (3), 250- 263.

Ediger, Marlow, and D. Bhaskara Rao (2006), *Successful School Education*. New Delhi, India: Discovery Publishing House.

Eisner, Elliot, (2006), "The Satisfactions of Teaching", *Educational Leadership*, 63 (6), 44-47.

Gulhane, G.L. (2006), "Rethinking Effective Teaching, Need of the Day", *Edutracks*, 5 (12),5-6. Published in India.

Hueser, Daniel, (2005), "Learning Logs: Writing to Learn, Reading to Assess", *Science and Children*, 43 (3), 46-49.

Liang, Lauren Aimonette, and Janice A. Dole (2006), "Help with Teaching Reading Comprehension: Instructional Frameworks", *The Reading Teacher*, 59 (8), 742-752.

Social Education, (2006), "Technology Position Statement and Guidelines", National Council for the Social Studies, 70 (5), 329-332.

6

WHAT MAKES FOR EFFECTIVE TEACHING IN SCHOOLS?

Good teachers are always in demand for all levels of instruction. They have a strong impact on assisting students to achieve well. Capable teachers can make tremendous contributions in any classroom of learners. Individual differences among students need to be studied and then provision made for each to attain optimally. A variety of appropriate learning activities need to be in the offing to assist students to do well in all curriculum areas. The writer supervised student teachers and co-operating teachers for thirty years in the public schools. His observations and recent literature on effective teaching will be used as content in this manuscript.

THE NEED FOR GOOD TEACHING

Which school does not want the best teachers available? The answer is, "They all want quality teachers who care for student achievement in all facets of development". How might school districts secure good teachers? First of all, interviewers need to secure teacher credentials from the teacher placement bureau of the supplying college/ university. They need to look for personal characteristics in the placement papers which meet needs of students. The placement papers will indicate what writers of the recommendations believe about the prospective teacher.

Each contributor to the credentials will write how he/she perceives the candidate in terms of contributing to leaner achievement. There are also boxes to check on qualities of the candidate. The credentials probably provide an overview of the candidates teaching potential. It is important to see the teacher actually teach in the school setting. The candidate reveals much more of teaching strengths in actual teaching than in what is written in his/her credentials. Even then, the observation will deal with a very short period of time in actual teaching. Persistence and duration is not assessed. Making quality decisions in teacher employment is of utmost importance and yet scanty data is used in noticing the strengths and weaknesses of candidates for a position.

Once teachers are employed, information may be secured for inservice education programs. Teachers need to prepare well for each day of teaching. The objectives section of the daily lesson plan need to be clearly stated. They need to be relevant and indicate salient knowledge for learner attainment. Three kinds of objectives need to be stressed such as knowledge, skills, and attitudinal ends. Rational balance among the three must be emphasized. Students, in the curriculum, then need to do well in many areas of growth and development. Learning opportunities to achieve the chosen objectives need to be varied and provide for individual levels of achievement. They need to secure the interests of children. Boredom and frustration should definitely not be a part of student learning. Appraisal procedures to ascertain student achievement need to be valid and reliable. They also should be diagnostic to provide feedback from students to the teacher pertaining to what students have left to learn.

Second, good teachers are able to obtain the attention of learners when teaching. It does little good if students are ignoring what is being taught. Rather, students should be stimulated to achieve the ongoing objectives of instruction. Methods of teaching should emphasize the psychology of learning. The psychology of learning emphasizes standards to use in teaching and learning which make for optimal learner achievement. Engagement of students in the ongoing social studies unit is necessary! Teachers need to observe students continually to notice if each is paying attention to adequately benefit from instruction. The teacher's voice in using stress, pitch, and juncture properly with involved voice inflection might well assist students to be more fully engaged in the ongoing unit of study.

Third, a variety of materials of instruction must be used. Students learn in different ways and these differences need adequate provision. For example, selected students prefer to work in committees to learn effectively. Thus within a small group, students may discuss subject matter and come up with viable conclusions. Other learners prefer to work individually on an assignment or project. Individually, students have their preferences be it in working collectively or by the self in achieving as optimally as possible.

Fourth, good sequence needs to be in the offing. Learning opportunities then must be ordered appropriately so that each learner experiences success in ongoing lessons and units of study. Each experience ideally should provide readiness for the ensuing learning activity. Failure to attain readiness hinders the next level of achievement. Background experiences are always necessary to understanding the new learnings. Quality experiences need provision so that each student may benefit more optimally from the new activity. Students may be motivated to raise questions as well as discuss possible answers pertaining to the new objective to be achieved. Or, the teacher may supply the needed learnings deductively.

Fifth, The talents of each student need to be used in teaching and learning situations. These talents include the following:

- abstract learning involving reading and writing
- logical thinking as in mathematics
- objective thought used to gather information
- psychomotor learning as in project methods of instruction
- artistic skills involving art activities
- inter-personal skills involving personal choices made in the curriculum
- interpersonal abilities as in small group decision making
- musical intelligence in setting words to music in ongoing lessons and units of study.

From the above named intelligences, it is quite apparent that many abilities may be used in developing quality lessons and units in teaching and learning situations. Thus reading, higher levels of cognition, hands on approaches, art work, and musical activities may be brought into large group, committee endeavours, and individual study with indepth learning. The talents of each student need to be used in the instructional arena. An integrated curriculum may then be stressed as well as ample time provided in teaching the separate subjects.

ADDITIONAL FACTORS TO EMPHASIZE

The teacher needs to be a good manager in the classroom. He/she needs to be highly knowledgeable about placing students in the proper group within a classroom to optimize instructional achievement. Large and small groups need to be formed when this optimizes achievement of students. At other times, students will be working by themselves individually. Flexible grouping must be stressed, but at all times the needs and abilities of the learner come foremost. The strengths of students need to be emphasized in certain grouping situations. At other times, the student needs placement whereby diagnosis and remediation are in emphasis. It is best if achievement is seamless in sequence, but there are times when the teacher needs to view specific errors of students and then re-teach what is needed.

There are diverse procedures which are recommended in grouping situations. These include the following conceptual plans:

- ungrading the curriculum
- an inter-disciplinary curriculum
- a multi-cultural emphasis
- peer groups and peer teaching
- heterogeneous and homogenous groups
- learning centers and student decision-making
- direct instruction as well as discovery learning.

Each of the above named plans should be studied indepth and, if implemented, with the needs of the learner in mind. Students are placed in groups to enhance learning and not for the sake of stressing a particular plan of grouping.

INSERVICE EDUCATION OF TEACHERS

Diverse plans of inservice education need to be assessed critically before putting them into practice. They must meet accepted criteria for improved teaching and learning situations. Innovations in teaching assist learners to achieve relevant objectives of instruction. They guide learners to attain specific objectives. Quality knowledge, skills, and attitudinal ends are emphasized in the innovation. Balance among these three categories of objectives need to be in the offing. Learning opportunities are aligned with the stated objectives. They stress relationship of different subject matter areas. Respect and acceptance of diverse cultures is emphasized. Committee endeavours as well as self-chosen activities are provided. Suggestions are provided for enrichment experiences as well as motivational activities. Direct teaching is emphasized so that students achieve key ideas and generalizations. Learning by discovery as well as inductive thinking is inherent in selected learning experiences. Learnings are properly ordered to provide for quality sequence.

Evaluation techniques need to be formative through the following assessment procedures:

- teacher written test items which are valid and reliable
- teacher observation, check lists, and rating scales
- teacher and student self-evaluations using appropriate criteria

Formative evaluations are used along the way as a unit of study is being taught. The teacher may then make needed changes as the unit progresses. Feedback to the teacher and students may be immediate so that strengths and weaknesses may be assessed in the instructional arena.

Summative evaluations are made at the close of a teaching unit. They may include the same/similar techniques of evaluation as those listed above for formative assessments. Mandated tests generally are considered as end of unit or summatzive evaluations. They may be mandated by the state or the local school district. Mandated tests may be used as formative evaluations if they provide feedback to the teacher as to what to re-teach or stress in ongoing learning opportunities. However, their results generally come back several months after the tests have been given.

REFERENCES

Boyd-Batstone, Paul (2004), "Focused Anecdotal Records Assessment: A Tool for Standards-Based, Authentic Assessment", *The Reading Teacher*, 58 (3), 230-239.

Darling-Hammond, Linda, and Barnett Berry (2006), "Highly Qualified Teachers for All", *Educational Leadership*, 64 (3), 14-20.

Ediger, Marlow (2006), "Motivational Efforts to Improve the Curriculum", *Iowa Educational Leadership* (ASCD), 9 (2), 19-21.

Ediger, Marlow, and D. Bhaskara Rao (2006), *Issues in School Curriculum*. New Delhi, India: Discovery Publishing House.

7

TUTORS FOR STUDENTS IN SCHOOLS

Tutors for public school students under the No Child Left Behind (NCLB) law will need to be chosen carefully so that those tutored are able to achieve, develop, and grow, as optimally as possible. If a school has failed to meet adequate yearly progress (AVP) criteria two years in a row, a student is entitled to free tutoring experiences in reading and in mathematics. Quality tutors need to be selected. Which criteria should tutors possess? This paper will discuss needed tutors in reading instruction.

QUALITY TUTORS FOR STUDENTS

There are a plethora of criteria which tutors need to possess. Students to be tutored need to fulfill expectations in terms of AVP as determined by the local state. They also need to meet promotion expectations of NCLB. Tutoring has grown to a billion dollar industry and expectations for tutoring services should be high.

To assist students in reading, the tutor needs to have a good knowledge of literacy instruction. Tutors for reading need to possess the following qualifications:

- ❖ having a baccalaureate degree with a minor, as a minimum, in the Teaching of Reading
- ❖ possessing adequate knowledge of diagnosis and remediation in reading difficulties
- ❖ being very knowledgeable of diverse plans of teaching reading such as Reading Recovery
- ❖ having much knowledge about students developing word analysis as well as comprehension skills
- ❖ being kind, considerate, and respectful of learners
- ❖ possessing enthusiasm and interest in tutoring (Ediger and Rao, 2001)

First of all, the tutor needs to ascertain the present achievement level of the tutee. This is a starting point for tutoring. There are standardized tests available to determine the present reading level of the child. However, it is not necessary to use standardized tests for this purpose. The tutor may begin with reading materials available and locate a book in which the student can pronounce, approximately, ninety-five per cent of the words correctly and answer three of four questions correctly covering subject matter read. Finding the starting point need not take much time since a skilled tutor should have much knowledge of tutoring and reading instruction. However, it is vital that the tutor determine the appropriate place for beginning reading instruction (Ediger, 1995).

The tutor needs to observe carefully and record the kinds of reading errors made. Common errors made by students include the following:

- ❖ omitting words when reading. This is especially harmful if the meaning of the text changes due to word omission.
- ❖ substituting a word for the correct word in the text. The content of the text material should not change. Word substitution generally makes for changes in meaning.
- ❖ repeating words read correctly. This is a habit which needs to be changed. The tutor may cover the words read correctly with a sheet of paper so that the student does not re-read that which was read correctly.
- ❖ skipping lines of print while reading. A sheet of paper may be used to move from the line read to the next sequential line.
- ❖ hesitating on words while reading. Successful practice in reading can make for avoidance of hesitations. Fluency in reading subject matter comes from re-reading some of the selections.
- ❖ reading in a jerky manner. Fluency in reading must be stressed for quality comprehension to take place. Having enough background information as well as' practice in reading a given selection might assist in taking care of problems relating to fluent reading (See Ediger, 2000).

The tutor needs to keep accurate record of common reading problems for a student and notice sequentially if progress is being made to alleviate difficulties. Each meeting date needs to be dated with clear records kept to make comparisons between past and present dates of observances of student reading. The tutor needs to be respectful of the tutee with no signs of rudeness, but acceptance of the other needs to be in the offing. A pleasant business like environment facilitates reading progress. Improved performance of the tutee should be expected with quality tutoring.

The importance of tutoring may be stated with the following:

> . . . specialized, tailored, and personalized educational services are becoming more and more attractive. For those who cannot afford full time private schooling, tutoring has emerged as a viable alternative. No study conclusively shows that tutoring boosts school achievement, but parents are wiling to pay for services that reduce the perceived risk of educational failure, even if those services have not been proven to be effective. This reasoning is further illustrated of evidence that the tutoring clientele is on average getting younger. As the tutoring market penetrates into younger age groups, its services further transcend the narrow structure of shadow education. When parents purchase these services for their younger children, they are taking a long range outlook, because the ultimate role of post secondary education lies far in the future.

The general culture of competition and its longer hopes are fueling the market for tutoring despite the latter's uncertain dividends. For an increasing number of families, tutoring has become a core competitive strategy, one that is affordable relative to other private alternatives. Tutoring franchises are responding to this growing demand with increasingly standardized services (Davies and Aurini, 2006).

. . . IRA's (International Reading Association) study of the research on quality classroom teachers of reading reveal that they possess the following skills:

- ❖ They understand children's reading and writing development

- They assess a child's individual progress and relate reading instruction to a child's previous experience
- They use a variety of ways to teach reading
- They use a variety of materials and texts for children to read
- They specifically tailor instruction to individual students.

Teachers must be adequately prepared to competently perform these various roles. IRA has articulated standards for five distinct categories of reading professionals responsible for reading instruction; paraprofessionals, classroom teachers, reading specialists, reading teacher educators, and administrators.

IRA firmly believes that students at all academic levels deserve access to high quality teachers who are trained in the teaching of reading. The association hopes to promote expanded adolescent literacy programs and to encourage professional development opportunities for teachers in the upper elementary grades and above who are involved in reading instruction, either as reading teachers or through content area reading (Reading today, 2006).

There are numerous reasons for having the best tutors possible for school age children. NCLB tests need to be passed. Promotion to the next higher grade level is a second goal and third, preferred vocations/professions require good readers for the better paying positions. Recreational reading, too, is important to enrich life and living.

REFERENCES

Davies, Scott, and Janice Aurini (2006), "The Franchising of Private Tutoring; a View from Canada", *Phi delta Kappan*, 88 (2),123-128.

Ediger, Marlow (1995), "Demonstration Teaching in the Schools", *Education*, 114 (2), 371-372.

Ediger, Marlow (2000), "Phonics and Poetry in the Curriculum", *Experiments in Education*, 28 (8),131-135.

Ediger, Marlow, and D. Bhaskara Rao (2001), *Teaching Reading Successfully*. New Delhi, India: Discovery Publishing House.

International Reading Association (2006), "High Quality Teachers: Strengthening Reading Requirements", *Reading Today*, 24 (2), 8.

8

HOMEWORK, INNOVATION AND SCHOOL

There is considerable debate pertaining to how helpful homework is in aiding student achievement. Does homework assist students to achieve more optimally? Selected educators say that well planned student homework related to what is studied in school will help students progress more rapidly. Others say that students need time to relax, rest, and engage in play activities instead.

There are certain criteria which the writer indicates need to be followed by teachers when requiring homework for students. These criteria will be discussed this paper.

CRITERIA FOR HOMEWORK ASSIGNMENTS

Assigning homework "because it is the thing to do" will rarely make, for increased learner achievement. Rather, there needs to be a purpose for students doing homework. Reasons do exist for having students participate in selected activities. Thus, there are reasons for doing homework. The following purposes appear to be salient for students:

- ❑ by doing more work in borrowing from the hundreds' column, increased meaning will be attached to the process
- ❑ by reading/reporting on a library book on the Crusades, the learner will learn indepth on events during the Middle Ages
- ❑ by voluntarily making a leaf collection of deciduous trees in fall, the student will increase interest on what happens when leaves change colour.

Prior to assigning homework, the teacher must think of student purposes for doing so. These need to be communicated to and accepted by the learner. Individual differences among learners must be provided for in order that each may attain as much as possible. Thus, all categories of students need assistance to achieve vital objectives of instruction. Vardell *et al.* (2006) indicated the following in matching books and other learning activities with English Language Learners (ELL):

- ❑ *Content Accessibility*. Is the story or topic familiar or helpful? When students already know about a concept in their language, transitioning a book in English about the same concept is not so overwhelming because they have a knowledge base upon which to build.
- ❑ *Language accessibility*. Is the language of the book simple and direct? Simple phrases or sentence patterns, a limited amount of text on each page, and predictable, repetitive text offer a reader friendly experience of English learners at a beginning proficiency level.
- ❑ *Visual Accessibility*. Are there abundant illustrations? When word knowledge is limited, readers rely on

other cues to help figure out the meaning of the text. This utilitarian function of illustrations is extremely helpful.

- ❑ *Genre Accessibility*. Are there a variety of genres available? Just as the classroom reflects diversity, the school and classroom library , should too—through a rich array of genres and topics.

Materials of instruction should be developmentally appropriate so the subject matter is understandable. Meaningful learnings are important for students. The above named criteria should be followed by teachers in matching library books and other materials of instruction with the child. This is true of doing homework as well as in the regular school curriculum. Developing purpose within learners is then more readily communicated.

In addition to purpose, students need to possess background information on the topic to be pursued as homework. Teachers need to be certain that learner's have the necessary knowledge to relate new ideas to be acquired with previous ideas gleaned. This makes for better sequence in learning. So often, students do poorly in homework because they do not possess prerequisite knowledge. An adult tends not read a novel or textbook on his/her own when not having the necessary background information. Possessing the prerequisite knowledge assists in making for meaningful learning. The student chooses to read a library book because possessed prerequisite knowledge makes the contents beneficial or interesting (Ediger and Rao, 2003).

Success in learning is vital. The teacher needs to present a model of using salient tenets of psychology in teaching and learning situations. Learning activities should definitely not be too difficult to make for students failing in course-work, nor too easy to make for boredome. But, pupils need to be wholeheartedly involved in the ongoing learning experiences. Not attending actively to a teaching/learning situation prevents a child from achieving more optimally. Being thoroughly engaged in learning is sign that achievement is taking place. Then too, a pupil must feel success in learning. The baseline for a learner is to begin where he/she is presently in achievement and then sequentially make continuous progress. Good sequence in learning experiences helps the pupil to relate the new with the previous learning. Previous knowledge and skills should provide the needed prerequisites to attain the new ends of instruction Success in doing homework should invite more voluntary efforts to achieve on one's own (Ediger, 2006).

Technology use has become an important way of providing for individual differences. Schools in today's digital age are filled with students who everyday retrieve archived information with a mouse click or stream video footage of events occurring around the world right into their classroom computers. In these same schools, millions of students cannot benefit as fully as possible from their education programs because of learning disabilities. Besides providing new ways to communicate, digital technologies can be a lifeline to this latter group...

As more of these students are being educated in inclusive classrooms, where they are expected to perform grade level work but not given specialized support, teachers are searching for ways to educate students with disabilities more effectively. Yet, too many teachers are unaware of the potential of assistive technologies to empower students struggling to work independently at their grade level (Hasselbring and Bausch, 2006).

Continuous ways need to be sought in having students use technology to do in school as well as homework. Technology has been the wave of the future and will continue to be so. It behooves the teacher to be highly cognizant of computer knowledge and skills to assist students to use technology to achieve objectives of instruction.

In using technology as well as new, desired ways of instruction, the following need to be implemented:

1. Create an innovating environment. Districts must reshape their organizational structures and systems to spark the process of innovating and to sustain innovations. Five actions are critical to make this happen:
   - ❑ Adapt school design that embody innovations, operating at or beyond the boundaries of curriculum practice. This is edge to - middle change.
   - ❑ Develop onto individual schools the creation of innovative programs and practices that substantially affect student learning and influence policy.
   - ❑ Make the innovations transparent to all, particularly the community.
   - ❑ Create systematic innovations that integrate schooling, health, housing, and neighbourhood revitalization.
   - ❑ Redesign system budget processes to accommodate the ways that small schools achieve economies of scale...
2. Focus on results, but not the same results for everyone.

3. Establish a culture for innovating.
4. Create true alternatives to prevailing practice (Washor and Mojkowski, 2006).

Changes made in schools need to follow desired criteria of teaching and learning. They must be made to harmonize with positive innovations in society. New ways must be found to make homework interesting for students. Understanding of what is learned in homework is salient. Subject matter acquired must be integrated with learnings obtained during the regular school day. Use needs to be made of achieved homework objectives.

REFERENCES

Ediger, Marlow (2006), "Oral Communication and Mathematics", *Edutracks*, 6 (1), 10-11. Published in India.

Ediger, Marlow, and D. Bhaskara Rao (2003), *Psychology and Curriculum*. New Delhi, India: Discovery Publishing House.

Hasselbring, Ted S., and Margaret E. Bausch (2006), "Assistive Technologies for Reading", *Educational Leadership*, 63(4), 72-75.

Vardell, Sylvia M., et. al. (2006), "Matching Books and Readers: Selecting Literature for English Learners, *The Reading Teacher*, (2006), 59(8),734-741.

Washor, Elliot, and Charles Mojlowski (2006), "Creating New Steps: Innovating from the Edge to the Middle", *Phi delta Kappan*, 87(10), 735-739.

9

LEADERSHIP IN SCHOOLS

It takes strong leaders to bring about positive changes in the elementary, middles schools, and high schools. Leaders are able to engage others in improving objectives of study, learning opportunities to achieve the stated objectives, as well as evaluation procedures. Designated leaders are the superintendent of schools, principals, curriculum directors, and department chair persons, among others. Their roles are generally well defined in terms of duties and responsibilities in respective leadership roles.

But what is the role of classroom teachers in providing leadership in improving the curriculum?

TEACHERS AS LEADERS

The classroom teacher may provide innumerable leadership roles in working toward improved teaching and learning situations. He/she makes many decisions in every-day classroom procedures. How should pupils be grouped for instruction? There can be the class as a whole, small groups/committees, and individualized study. When to use which procedure depends upon what assists pupils to achieve most optimally. Then too, there may be homogenous and heterogeneous plans of grouping for instruction. There are a plethora of additional decisions to be made such as the length of time devoted to each procedure as well as the sequence in individual learning activities (Ediger, 2007).

There are many contributions, teachers may make toward the larger picture of curriculum improvement. A teacher or team may volunteer to assist in inservice education programs. Thus, a plan may be developed and approved pertaining to improving reading instruction. Objectives of the inservice education program might well include the role of phonics in providing for individual differences among learners. There are numerous issues in teaching phonics such as assisting learners as the need arises in an ongoing reading experiences as compared to teaching phonics prior to its actual use. Also, the intensity of phonics teaching needs clarification. Might sequential phonic learnings be developed within a complete unit of study in reading instruction? How should the use of context clues to ascertain unknown words be emphasized? Opposite of using these word recognition techniques in teaching reading is the Big Book approach. Beginning instruction, here, stresses holism in reading content together by pupils with teacher guidance. This is followed by pupils reading content individually (See Landsman and Gorski, 40-44).

What then should be the role of phonics instruction in providing for individual differences among pupils in learning to read? Which parts of each of the following plans for teaching reading may be used to exemplify a quality program of reading instruction?

- a basal reading program with accompanying manual

- individualized reading using library books
- programmed reading with computer use
- reciprocal reading as well as questioning the author (QtA)
- Success for All (developed by Robert Slavin)
- scripted reading such as the Open Court series.

With the above named plans, teacher(s) conducting an inservice program need to assist participants to analyze each program. Brain storming may be one approach to use here. Conclusions need to be developed in reaching consensus from the brain storming activity as to which ingredients to use in coming up with the best procedure of reading instruction possible. An improved reading curriculum should result. Selected items from the brain storming experience might then be incorporated into the present program of instruction. If possible, it is good for the teacher to report back to the inservice participants how the change was perceived by pupils in the classroom (See Ortlieb, *et al.*, 2007).

ISSUES IN THE READING CURRICULUM

There are salient issues which teachers need to discuss. Sometimes, what was accepted as being "good" becomes an issue later. In the remediation arena, the following are considered as a basis for diagnosis and remedial teaching:

- a child repeating a word or phrase read correctly. This may be done by the reader to determine accuracy of what was read.
- looking back at what was read correctly. This might be done to check if the oral reading was done correctly.

- reading a word or phrase haltingly. This may occur when the reader is reading in a reflective manner.

Each of the above must be evaluated by the teacher to ascertain if fluency in reading is lacking or if there is an involved purpose in clarifying a purpose. When pupils substitute words for those in actual print, the teacher needs to notice if this distorts the meaning of the sentence. It may not be a serious error if sentence meaning remains intact. Otherwise, a more careful approach to word recognition must be stressed. These approaches may include the use of context clues, phonics, and syllabication analyses. Looking back at what was read might indicate the child is reflecting upon what was read to make certain of the accuracy of content read. In all cases, it is important to read as fluently as possible (See Gammill, 2006).

For inservice eduction, teacher leadership might well be involved in discussing the following:

- What is meant by fluency in reading?
- Should decoding skills be taught prior to a reading activity, or should they be taught as the need arises?
- What role does reflective thinking play in reading?
- How might pupils best reveal comprehension of what was read?
- How much emphasis should be placed upon peer learning in order to assist pupils in word recognition as well as in higher order of thinking skills?

A PROFESSIONAL LIBRARY FOR TEACHERS

Teachers may show leadership skills by assisting in establishing a professional library. A good approach in inservice education which is ongoing is for teachers to work co-operatively in developing a professional library for teachers. The professional library may be used within an inservice education program or separately as teachers have time to read professional literature in the teaching of reading. During school time or at home, reading the professional books should have as an objective for teachers to improve reading instruction. Professional textbooks in the teacher's library should contain content in the following areas of instruction:

- diverse work recognition/decoding skills
- whole language experiences for children
- an integrated curriculum
- different plans in teaching reading
- means of assessing/evaluating learner achievement and progress
- organizing the reading curriculum
- innovations in reading instruction
- developing wholesome attitudes
- developmental programs in teaching and learning
- creative approaches in teaching reading.

Professional books in the teaching of reading may be ordered on the internet. There are several periodicals, as a minimum, which should also be an inherent part of a professional library for teachers; these are the following with the publishing company listed in parenthesis:

- The Language Arts (The National Council Teachers of English)
- The Reading Teacher (The International Reading Association)
- Educational Leadership (The Association for Supervision and Curriculum Development)

- Phi Delta Kappan (Phi Delta Kappa).

Teachers must have time to analyze and discuss literature pertaining to the teaching of reading. Critical and creative thinking as well as problem solving need to be involved. Making use of ideas read and sharing these with colleagues is important in inservice education (Ediger, 2003).

DEVELOPING GRADE LEVEL MEETINGS

As a university supervisor of student teachers, the writer spoke with the principal of a participating school who stated that grade level meetings begun two years ago had truly stimulated improved instruction. The teachers established goals, meeting dates, and kept a running account of what transpired.

A team of teachers might then work with others on the same grade level or in a combination of grades such as the primary or intermediate grades. The mechanics and logistics for each meeting should be co-operatively determined. Within these meetings, problems in teaching should be discussed such as the following:

- developing and maintaining pupil interest among special needs children
- motivating learners to achieve
- establishing purpose for learning
- helping struggling readers
- assisting English Language Learners (ELL)
- teaching pupils to attain mandated objectives
- seeking a commercial reading program to help learners progress (Ediger and Rao, 2007).

Minutes of each meeting should be kept and distributed among school personnel. Sharing of ideas among grade levels is important. They might well be tried out in different classrooms with feed back provided to the involved group. Methods of inservice education should be a motivating factor to improve reading instruction!

IMPLICATIONS FOR FURTHER RESEARCH

Although this paper represents an initial effort to examine the personal characteristics of educational leaders that appear to facilitate the implementation of school improvement interventions for at-risk students, it has also fostered questions regarding the personal characteristics needed of the leaders involved in these efforts. The following questions are implications for further research.

Do the characteristics discussed represent a composite picture of leaders of educational change or are there other characteristics that have not surfaced?

Is there a unique formula for these characteristics that educators attempting to implement an educational innovation or a systemic change at the school or district level should seek to possess?

Does having congruent values between a community and a superintendent promote and encourage school improvement?

What is the influence of leaders' values and beliefs on their leadership skills?

Can these characteristics be learned or are they innate? If they can be acquired, how does this occur?

This paper represents an initial attempt to identify the characteristics of leaders who initiate, guide, and provoke school change. Six common characteristics were found in superintendents, principals, and teachers who have experienced the adventure of school change. The data discussed in this synthesis is timely considering current endeavors to restructure districts and schools. Further research attempting to answer the questions that have emerged from this literature review will further our understanding of what types of individuals can lead the needed school reforms as well as provide information on whether or not these characteristics can be acquired throughout an educator's career. The possibility of being able to acquire and use these characteristics holds great promise for those participating in and leading the educational reforms of today.

REFERENCES

Ediger, Marlow (2007), "Teacher Observation to Assess Learner Achievement", *Journal of Instructional Psychology*, 34 (3), 137-139.

Ediger, Marlow (2003), "Data Driven Decision Making", *College Student Journal*, 37 (1), 9-15.

Ediger, Marlow, and D. Bhaskara Rao (2007), *Reading Curriculum and Instruction*. New Delhi, India: Discovery Publishing House.

Landsman, Julie, and Paul Gorski (2007), "Countering Standardization", *Educational Leadership*, 64 (8), 40-44.

Gammill, Deidra M. (2006), "Learning the Write Way", *The Reading Teacher*, 59 (8), 754-763.

Ortlieb, Evan, *et al.* (2007), The Art of Reading: Dramatizing Literacy", *Reading Improvement*, 44 (3), 169-176.

10

LEADERS IN SCHOOLS

Where should public school leaders be trained to become principals, supervisors, and superintendents? Traditionally, schools of education in universities have been responsible for training school administrators. This notion has been challenged by those advocating alternative choices for administrators in schools. Thus, the business and military world have advocated their being able to provide needed leadership in the public schools. This paper will analyze diverse procedures in providing leaders for the education of students.

UNIVERSITY PREPARED SCHOOL ADMINISTRATORS

Historically, university schools of education have trained and educated personnel for becoming school administrators. They, usually, have received a BSE degree to teach in the classroom setting. By taking appropriate course work and engaging in related field experiences in an approved university, the student might receive a graduate degree as well as certification in becoming a school administrator. The needed degree may be an Sp Ed or a Doctorate, in school administration. Course work may include the following:

- classes in school administration, supervision, and curriculum with emphasis placed upon research, theory, trends, and practice
- a practicum including shadowing public school administrators, discussing problems and issues with these principals/superintendents, as well as filling in on administrative duties
- seminars and conferences with the university supervisor
- maintaining a portfolio pertaining to the internship in school administration
- passing the comprehensive examination in the work of a principal or superintendent
- meeting standards of an administrator's academy, such as in Missouri. These standards involve a doing approach of a variety of tasks which school administrators perform in the public schools.

Each of the above must stress quality in its offering. Thus, the role model to emulate in the school setting must be a dedicated, professional school administrator. He/she must be knowledgeable, skillful, and possess good, positive attitudes toward school administration. The co-operating school administrator in the public schools has exceptional knowledge of the curriculum as well as means to improve instruction in the school setting. He/she is able to work well with interns in a manner which truly prepares excellence in school administrators.

Reasons for advocating that schools of education in universities be in charge of preparing administrators of schools are the following:

- involved professors have much training and education in the preparation of principals and superintendents
- these professors have been former school administrators and understand issues and problems therein
- they have been former classroom teachers and have experienced teaching and learning as well as inservice education programs to improve instruction
- they have experienced working with parents on curricular matters
- they also have been heavily involved in parent/ teacher conferences
- they have been leaders in providing inservice education for teachers (Ediger and Rao, 2006).

The above pertain to ideals which school administrators should possess. Elmore (2006), wrote the following:

> Thanks to Arthur Levine's report, Educating School Leaders, it is no longer necessary to belabour the catastrophe that is the education, certification, and licensure of school leaders in the US. The cartel—the inter-locking and self-perpetuating system of state agencies, cash for credit university programs, and hopelessly inadequate local hiring practices—has been exposed once again in all its gory detail, this time from within.
>
> The issue now is what should be done about it. I am dubious about universities getting better without first competing for the franchise. Rather, I think, we need to rebuild a system of preparation of school leaders.

EXECUTIVES FROM THE BUSINESS WORLD AS SCHOOL ADMINISTRATORS

There have been advocates who believe in the business world providing leadership in schools as school administrators. Advocates state that school leadership and executive officers in the business world are congruent in many ways. They believe that management of the two domains are similar. Business world management principles are necessary where billions of dollars are involved in paying costs for educating of public school pupils. Money needs to be budgeted and spent intelligently. Achievement of students needs to be upped and harmonize with moneys spent. Additional reasons given in using management procedures in school operations include the following:

- education is a business and executives from the business world must be in charge
- efficiency is a key concept in school operations; public moneys are not to be wasted
- measurement results are needed from students to show achievement. Standardized tests are good indicators of learner progress
- data from student test score printouts provide a basis for curricular decision-making. Thus, data driven decision making must be in the offing
- measurable student results can be graphed to show gains in achievement. This is comparable to showing profits in the business world.
- competition among schools are to be encouraged through publishing report cards in newspapers of school achievement.

There are questions which need studying and answering pertaining to business management procedures being applicable to public school progress. The business world stresses the free enterprise system and capitalism, whereas the public domain is emphasized in governing the public schools. The former stresses the bottom line which is the profit motive. Public schools do not stress the profit motive, but they are open to scrutiny such as school board meetings being open to public participation. No business is to be discussed in secret, expect for discussions on personnel. Minutes of school board meetings are open to viewing by responsible persons. Business management procedures very readily would involve contracts with companies which privatize and manage schools for profit. The profit motive might move in the direction of eliminating faculty and staff to increase corporate profits. Food and janitorial services may also find fewer being employed to increase profits. The following need indepth answers:

- are management procedures applicable to the education of students?
- can the profit motive be harmonized with optimal student achievement?
- are test scores to be harmonized with revealing student achievement?
- test scores are "objective", but should other more subjective means, such as portfolios, also be used to ascertain learner progress?
- do tests really measure what is important to acquire such as acceptance of others, civility, politeness, and humanness?
- does competition make for rivalry among and between school personnel?

- will Chief Executive Officers' salaries, bonuses, and benefits cipher off too much money in terms of educating students?

A major question pertains to business management procedures being applied to situations where these leaders have had no knowledge and experience of curriculum development and design (See, Mc Tighe and O'Connor, 2005).

LEADERS FROM THE MILITARY BEING SCHOOL ADMINISTRATORS

Advocates of the military becoming school administrators has had selected advocates. These military personnel have reached a high rank such as being generals and colonels in the army, air force, or marines, as well as admirals in the navy. They have been leaders in the military and have revealed competence in leadership abilities. Advocates believe that leadership in one domain equals leadership in others. The late Casper Wineberger, secretary of defense in the Reagan Administration, was a strong advocate of military personnel being leaders in working with young people in the school setting.

There are problems with having a military philosophy harmonizing with democratic ideals in teaching and learning. Military leaders and school administrators might well involve two different kinds of personnel with little congruence between the two. Thus, leadership in one domain may not equal that in another area of life. Then too, the military is based upon a command system. Orders are given from top down in a hierarchical manner. The goals of military training are quite different from that of education in the civilian school setting. The former stresses protecting the borders of the nation using whatever means are at hand whereas the latter's goals emphasize the importance of preparing citizens to live in a democratic society.

It was focused upon three sources to provide leadership in the public school setting. These were presented in terms of goals stressed by each source. Educators must continually study objectives of administration from a plethora of sources. There may be learnings to be secured from non-traditional sources which are applicable to school administration. Making attacks on traditional sources must be made based up research, philosophical thinking, and quality criteria. The question remains, "Under which conditions do students learn best?" School administrators need to:

- possess quality attitudes toward teaching and learning institutions .
- be wise managers of resources available for schooling
- excel as leaders of faculty and personnel
- have good working relations with parents
- show the highest respect for minority groups
- harmonize efforts with other societal groups in working for the well being of young people
- be advocates for appropriate buildings, equipment, and teaching aids which focus upon quality teaching
- assist in providing necessary inservice education for teachers and support staff
- promote purchasing and using technology in the school setting. This should assist students to live effectively in school and in society (Ediger and Rao, 2003).

REFERENCES

Ediger, Marlow, and D. Bhaskara Rao (2006), *Effective School Education*. New Delhi, India: Discovery Publishing House.

Ediger, Marlow, and D. Bhaskara Rao (2003), *Elementary Curriculum*. New Delhi, India: Discovery Publishing House.

Elmore, Richard E. (2006), "Breaking the Cartel", *Phi Delta Kappan*, 87 (7), 513 -515.

Tighe, Jay, and Ken O'Connor (2005), "Seven Practices for Effective Learning", *Educational Leadership*, 63 (3), 10-17.

11

DISCIPLINE IN SCHOOLS

Teachers have frequently stated that discipline problems are a major problem in teaching students. Quality discipline is needed so that students may achieve as optimally as possible. If students are distracted from learning, they lose out on significant learnings. Later, in sequence, students may notice gaps possessed. Some will be due to not having paid attention in class. The teacher does have an obligation to prepare well for each lesson taught. Thus, he/she needs to engage students in ongoing learning experiences. The interests of students need to be secured. Meaningful learning must accrue so that students understand that which was taught. Also, purpose or reasons for achieving need to be emphasized. Then too, teachers must provide for individual differences in the classroom. There are then a plethora of specifics which teachers must attend to in teaching and learning situations. Students are attracted to teachers who have expert power (Ediger and Rao, 2007).

But a major problem remains and that is discipline or appropriate student behaviour. The public schools must accept all students who are of school age. These students will be future delinquents, felons, abusers, as well as upright, highly contributing members in society. Each student deserves the best curriculum possible.

Major schools of thought in discipline will be discussed in the balance of this manuscript. Hopefully, this will assist teachers and administrators in helping students to achieve well in school and in society.

SCHOOLS OF THOUGHT IN DISCIPLINE

Reinforcement theory emphasizes teachers rewarding what is positive behaviour in the classroom. Here, teachers need to be specific as to what is required of students. Thus, if students are to have a popcorn party on Friday afternoon, the specific behaviours need to be spelled out for participation, such as getting home work and school requirements in on time. If a student fails to meet the requirements, he/she may not participate in the popcorn party, unless there are legitimate reasons. The following are additional examples of students meeting precise, measurable requirements:

- not causing unnecessary disturbances in the classroom
- improving performance over previous efforts, in any academic area.

Teacher judgement always needs to be used in making disciplinary decisions. There are causes for happenings which affect student performance.

The writer supervised university student teachers in one school where there was a student teacher and a co-operating teacher in the same classroom with only thirteen students. This made it possible to do much reinforcing of student learning through a reward system. Thus, in an English learning through a reward system. Thus, in an English workbook lesson, student were working on filling in the blank space with the proper verb form. Students individually received a Santa Clause stamp for each of ten completion test items. The stamp (for December) was printed next to each correct response, immediately upon responding correctly. With two teachers and thirteen students, it was possible to immediately reward student learning. Reinforcement of the correct answer was then in evidence. The learner was either right or wrong in the answer given.

As another example, students individually were to receive a stick of chewing gum if they received 100% correct in spelling fifteen words correctly in a weekly test on Friday. Monday through Thursday, learning activities were presented to prepare students for the Friday test.

Reinforcement theory places major emphasis upon the response to a given situation. Thus, correct responses are desired from the learner and these are then rewarded. Situations should are set up as learning activities whereby the student can be successful. Success provides opportunities for positive feelings to be stressed with a reward. Rewards may be material as in a small prize; verbal such as praise; and/or non-verbal—a smile from the teacher, gesture, or facial expression. Students then abide by the teacher's decisions due to personal power possessed by the teacher. Rewards given by the teacher may be satisfying at the same time (Guilfoyle, 2006).

Second, the teacher presents a model for students to emulate in good behaviour. Thus, the teacher works well with children in the classroom in providing quality instruction. Politeness and kindness abound as shown by the teacher. Students are aware that they come first in importance, above that of subject matter taught, as well as that of rules and regulations in the classroom.

The teacher must be an example for moral and ethical behaviour. Sometimes, the actions of teachers speak much louder than words. Thus, how the teacher works with students in teaching and learning situations is very salient! Attractive power emphasizes that students have positive attitudes toward the teacher and desire to fulfil requirements in achievement and learning (See Brassell 2006-2007).

Third, well qualified teachers assist in minimizing misbehaviour. They have much subject matter knowledge pertaining to what is taught as well as possessing appropriate methods-of teaching to actively engage learners. Students tend to respect teachers then who possess expert power. Teachers who do not have the necessary facts, concepts, and generalizations to teach an ongoing lesson or unit of study might well lose the confidence of learners and cause discipline problems. Well prepared teachers for each day of teaching is a necessity. Coercive power may need to be used at times when structural ideas need to be acquire by students, but it is better to use other more positive procedures and power in teaching.

There are times when the teacher uses preventative discipline techniques to avoid student misbehaviour. Thus, a teacher needs to analyze teaching and learning situations to ascertain what might cause discipline problems. For example, a long line of students in the lunch room waiting to be served tends to cause tension and might involve discipline problems among students. Being unrealistic in making assignments, for students to complete, might well be very frustrating to students. Students may not be able to complete what the teacher desires. This is annoying to standard need to be evaluated to avoid unfortunate student responses. Attempts at avoiding problems and yet having students achieve optimally is a noble objective in school discipline (See Duke, 2006).

Fourth, teachers and administrators need to study newer emphasized approaches on discipline which are recommendable procedures. Each school should have a professional library for teachers to read about innovations in education. Educational journals and university teacher education textbooks which are reputable should be immediately available to teachers for locating information on school discipline, among other sources / topics.

Selected procedures emphasized by educators in upholding school discipline standards include the following:

- assertive discipline (Lee Cantor)
- reality therapy (William Glasser)
- time out station
- detention time
- logical consequences approach.

Selected schools have adopted after school sessions for students not completing assignments during the school day. Each plan studied for remedying discipline problems requires originality in ascertaining the application of each in practical situations. Teachers and administrators, also, need be creative in thinking abut unique approaches in solving / minimizing discipline problems in the school setting.

Video tapes of teaching situations need to be available for teacher / administrator analyzing and answers sought for problems relating to discipline. There should be opportunities for teachers to visit classrooms where specific, reputable plans of discipline are used. Discussions should be used as follow-ups. Facets of what has been learned need to be tried out in the classroom and reports made in faculty meetings of the success of the innovation (Ediger, 2007).

Fifth, seminars need to be conducted whereby participants study indepth particular plans of discipline. Resource materials need to be available. The findings of a seminar need to be reported to other operating seminars. Ideas gained may, in part, may be implemented in the classroom. The lines of communication must be kept open to communicate results to participants. Experimentation is salient in gathering and using important ideas in improving classroom discipline.

Action research should be used to test innovations used as to their quality in improving the classroom environment. Classrooms need to be conducive to learning. With action research, data is obtained from the group with the treatment (new approach) versus the traditional method of disciplining learners. A pretest and a post-test needs to be given to each of the two groups. The pre-test should be used to equate the initial test results. Analysis of covariance may need to be used if the two groups differ significantly from each other. The results from the post-test need to be viewed as to which group achieves better academically in a quality learning environment (See, Unmesh, 2007).

Carefully choosing methods of discipline are salient in developing emotionally stable individuals. Cruelty and physical punishment should definitely be eliminated. Rather, a learning environment needs to be implemented which encourages learning and the development of a well rounded educated individual. It is also important to work with parents in emphasizing quality discipline in the school setting (Ediger, 2007).

REFERENCES

Brassell, Danny (2006-2007), "Inspiring Young Scientists with Great Books", *The Reading Teacher*, 60, (4), 336-343.

Duke, Daniel L. (2006), "What We Know and Don't Know About Improving Low Performing Schools", *Phi Delta Kappan*, 87 (10), 729-734.

Ediger, Marlow (2007), "Balance in the Curriculum", *College Student Journal*, 41 (2), 376-378.

Ediger, Marlow (2007), "Role of the School Administrator", *Experiments in Education*, 35 (5), 105-108. Published in India.

Ediger, Marlow, and D. Bhaskara Rao (2007), *Curriculum of School Subjects.* New Delhi, India; Discovery Publishing House.

Guilfoyle, Christy (2006), "NCLB; Is There Life Beyond Testing", *Educational Leadership*, 64 (3), 8-13.

Unmesh, Doctor. (2007), "Assuring Quality Teacher Education in Present Scenario", *Edutracks*, 6 (9), 13-19. Published in India.

12

SCHOOL AND STUDENTS IN SOCIETY

Students come from different socio-economic levels in society. Thus, they do not come to school with equivalent background experiences. Students from upper and middle class socio-economic communities do better in test results as compared to those who come from poverty homes. By viewing mandated test results, it is quite obvious that money assists in securing the good things in life such as tours of other nations/states as well as reading materials at home, and the possibilities of attending prestigious private schools and universities. Parents of higher income levels possess a higher level of educational attainment and do more reading at home which provides a good model for children. Better clothes for children, better homes, and the possibilities of healthful nutrition are further advantages of having adequate incomes. After school programs of lessons in different fields in music and dance further accentuates benefits of being in the upper income levels.

NATIONAL AND STATE OBJECTIVES FOR STUDENT ATTAINMENT

The No Child Left Behind (NCLB) federal law of 2002 emphasizes cognitive objectives, largely, for all students to attain on a specific grade level (grades three through eight and a high school exit test). For any grade level, students take the same test. This is generally true regardless of ability levels or cultural factors such as being a special needs student, an English Language Learner (ELL), or a student from a minority group. All take the same standardized grade level tests with the same time limits for test taking. Any separate category such as special needs children (mentally retarded students, for example) need to show adequate yearly progress or the entire school is deemed as "failing". It's a one size 'fits all' set of beliefs involved in testing (Ediger and Rao, 2007a).

More needs to be said about the home and environmental conditions which students experience from birth to and including the public school years. Those students who grow up in poverty have several strikes against them. They have not experienced models conducive to doing well in school. The late A.H. Maslow (1954), emphasized five general sequential needs of individuals in order to do well in life. The lowest level is for individuals to have adequate nutrition, sleep and rest, as well as have appropriate clothing.

The second level is for individuals to have safety needs met. Freedom from danger and abuse is important. The third level stresses having belonging needs met. All like to possess feelings of belonging. Being isolated and shunned does not make for happiness. Next, esteem needs must be met. Each person desires to be recognized for achievements made and not be bullied. For improved performance in school, all may have esteem needs met with praise and other forms of rewards for improved performance. Then too, individuals like to become the kind of person desired, as a final objective. Maslow's hierarchy of human needs provides a framework for goals which most individuals crave and wish. Too many students experience tremendous obstacles to success in school and in life generally. No Child Left Behind (NCLB) advocates seemingly believe that all students on a specific grade level can experience success regardless of the home and societal environment.

SELF-DIRECTED ACHIEVEMENT

Value added approaches in testing would better reveal an individual student's progress as compared to predetermined standards as advocated by NCLB. In valued added approaches, each student would be compared with his/her previous test score to ascertain achievement. Achievement for any student is desired rather than achievement of predetermined standards. The latter stresses a student setting out to achieve what a remote set of test makers believe that learners should achieve. In contrast, value added procedures emphasize a student's achievement over previous test results. Is growth in evidence?

Too many reports indicate that student's are drilled in reading and mathematics, the two areas of the curriculum presently being tested, in order to do well in passing to the next higher grade level as well as to meet adequate yearly progress (AVP). Science was added for the 2007-2008 school year. This still leaves out social studies, health and physical education, as well as art in the school curriculum. A well rounded education stresses more than two or three curriculum areas.

Then too with drill being stressed as a method of teaching, the psychology of learning is not being emphasized in teaching and learning situations. Strongly recommend that the instructional arena promote the following criteria for teachers to follow:

- emphasizes active involvement of students in learning. The student then is fully engaged in the learning process and not a passive recipient of knowledge and skills.
- stresses purpose in learning in that it assists learners to perceive the values inherent in achieving.
- builds self-confidence in the learner to be resilient in the face of obstacles
- motivates students to become intrinsically inclined to achieve, grow, and develop
- develops and explores student interests to attain relevant objectives of instruction
- emphasizes students developing self-efficacy in promoting self confidence within learners (Ediger and Rao, 2007).

A variety of rich learning experiences will assist students to develop optimally in diverse facets of achievement, be it in knowledge, skills, attitudes, morality, and ethics. Positive attitudes toward each learner will guide learners to feel humanely and wisely toward others.

THE CURRICULUM OF SCHOOL SUBJECTS

The school curriculum needs to develop talents of individuals fully. No talent should be wasted, but rather fulfilled in meeting personal desires and wishes. Teachers need to listen to their students to ascertain what they hope to learn as well as the means of learning. This still leaves ample time for achieving basic subject matter knowledge and skills. Questions which students have must be accepted as having worth and need adequate elaboration.

Many times, students reveal interests through the selection of library books to be read during Sustained Silent Reading (SSR). For those not reading well by the self, the teacher should read aloud fascinating library books during story time. Narrative, expository, and creative works (poetry) need to be inherent in the read aloud. The teacher may observe student interests and attention during this time. Also, a few stimulating questions may be raised following the read aloud. When reading aloud, the teacher must use proper voice inflection, pitch, and stress to capture learner attention. Library books for SSR and the read aloud need to be on a variety of genre and reading levels to provide for individual differences, with emphasis on the following:

- different kinds of work performed by individuals in the societal arena,
- bibliotherapy and how individuals overcame selected difficulties and problems,
- people in foreign lands with cultural likenesses and differences,
- natural disasters such as tornados, hurricanes, mudslides, earthquakes, among others, and how welfare and relief groups assist victims in these tragic times,
- the necessity of proper health care (medical, dental, and optical) for all in society,
- honesty in government to make for a viable democracy,

- identifying racial and other prejudices which hinder achievement of individuals in society
- helping the needy and less fortunate in the societal arena

Students need to engage in doing community service with appropriate supervision in safe places. Community service projects must stress relevant objectives, carefully chosen, and aimed at improving society. Readiness for each project needs to be in evidence so that lifelong participants will be developed. Thus, worthwhile learning opportunities will result in doing community service. A variety of developmentally appropriate activities to achieve objectives need to be in the offing.

Students need to learn about the local community through excursions, the internet, power point presentations, and from resource people in the community. Experiences pertaining to the community should be meaningful and encourage student life long learning. Through discussions, students may gain indepth learnings. Problems will be identified and answers sought using diverse reference sources. Students need to learn from first hand experiences as well as through semi-concrete and abstract learning activities. There are additional follow-up experiences which students might well experience, pertaining to community learning experiences such as:

- making a collage
- doing a report in class
- dramatizing the role of a worker in the community
- conducting a panel presentation on life in a community
- developing a bulletin board display on community helpers

- participating in a seminar on different levels of government
- reporting on a city ordinance
- committee work and report on penalties for law violations (See Parker, 2001).

Students should always be encouraged to do extra work such as volunteering to serve on writing a classroom newspaper. Each activity participated in should be appraised in terms of thoroughness, quality, effort put forth, and involved thought.

Virtual communities, due to technology use, has made it so that a distant place, or any area/region, may be brought right into the classroom. There is then no scheduling of buses and chaperones. Also, no appointments need to be made with the place of visitation. Programs allow students across country to visit a zoo, for example, without getting on the school bus. Behlmann wrote (August 27, 2007) the following:

> (Moultrie) Georgia students visited the Lee Richardson Zoo (Garden City, Kansas) on Wednesday—without ever leaving their seats. Ryan Schaffer held a screech owl for students to see, as part of a lesson on animals that fly.
>
> A ninth grader 1,300 miles away chimed in with a question, "Would the animal bite?"
>
> Schaffer, the distant learning co-ordinator at Lee Richardson Zoo, was confident it wouldn't.
>
> "The only time an animal will bite you if you hurt it or if it looks like its food", he said from the Finnup Center for Conservation Education at the zoo. The students followed Schaffer's lesson via video. . . . The zoo has been providing live programs for ten years. . . .

Technology has made it possible to bring live programs, even from remote areas, into the classroom. These virtual field trips emphasize reality and might well relate to almost any social studies/science unit of study being taught in the classroom setting. Virtual communities then can be brought into the classroom to stimulate interest and curiosity. School and society have been brought closer together via video.

REFERENCES

Behlmann, Emily (August 27, 2007), *Virtual Field Trips*, The Hutchinson, Kansas, News, A6.

Ediger, Marlow, and D. Bhaskara Rao (2007a), *Administration of Schools*. New Delhi, India: Discovery Publishing House.

Ediger, Marlow, and D. Bhaskara Rao (2007b), *Reading Curriculum and Instruction*. New Delhi, India: Discovery Publishing House, Chapter Five.

Maslow, A.H. (1954), *Motivation and Personality*. New York: Harper and Row.

Parker, Walter C. (2001), *Social Studies in Elementary Education*. Upper Saddle River, New Jersey: The Macmillan Company.

13

HOLISM, SCHOOL CAFETERIA AND STUDENTS

Eating meals in the school cafeteria should be a happy time to enjoy good food. Too frequently, pupils in the cafeteria talk loudly, shout, and throw food to make exchanges with others. A considerable amount of rudeness is in evidence. Time sent in the lunchroom is usually short since the next set of pupils from another classroom must take their turn in eating. Very often, twenty minutes per classroom is allowed from the time the classroom is left until it is time to leave the lunchroom after eating. Within that framework, what might the school do to encourage social growth and development?

GOOD BEHAVIOUR IN THE LUNCHROOM

Some of the misbehaviour is due to space considerations. If twenty minutes is allotted per classroom for pupils eating lunch, including leaving the classroom, following the line to be served, as well exiting, studies need to be made on what must be done to improve the situation. The following, needs to be studied, discussed and analyzed:

- can the time given to serving lunch be streamlined effectively? Creative minds working co-operatively can do much to identify and solve problems
- how might the waiting time for serving be less tedious? This may include straddling learners as they leave the classroom and come into the lunchroom sequentially in sets of five. This would cut down on misbehaviour in a line. Is it possible to arrange for an additional serving line for pupils to receive the noon meal?

Pupils, too, need to co-operate in securing their trays and sitting down at the table in an orderly approach. This may need to be modeled by teachers or the school principal for pupils to view clearly. Good table manners also need to be modeled. Thus, pupils need to see first hand what can be done to make for a mannerly lunchroom. All pupils should have opportunities to participate in lunchroom conversation. No one should dominate nor shun others from participating. Respect and acceptance of what others have to say is important. A caring community needs to be developed. Feelings of belonging in the lunchroom, and more specifically, in the conversational setting must be encouraged. There is a basic human need in wanting to be accepted in school and in society. A psychological need, such as feelings of belonging, may be met while incorporating good manners and enjoy eating lunch at the same time (Ediger and Rao, 2007).

Meeting esteem needs in the school cafeteria is salient. The whole person is then involved in learning. Thus, pupils individually or collectively may be praised for good behaviour. Good behaviour should encourage quality listening within a setting emphasizing conversation. In society, conversation is probably the most important oral communication experience. Then too, human beings like to be rewarded for things well done. Praise as a reward, in a plethora of cases, works well as reinforcement. Good conversation should then come forth with increased frequency.

School achievement and progress are increased when pupils respect each other. Bullying and harassment are greatly minimized, or ideally, omitted (See Hoyand Miskel, 2005).

School furniture also needs to be respected. Rules need to be developed and adhered to. Periodically, discussions need to be conducted on rules being followed as well as those being violated. Remedies for problems need to be sought. If lunchroom furniture is defaced, the kinds of defacement must be identified with ways found to remedy the situation.

LUNCH TIME IN SCHOOL

Pertaining to nutritional foods, Hutson (2007), wrote the following:

> It's lunchtime in school. Your student pulls out their lunch box or sack lunch and takes a look at what you've packed for the daily meal.
>
> What will they find? Will it be something they will want to keep or will they use your lunch entrees as trading materials for the latest junk food options?
>
> As long as students have been easting lunch at school, parents have been trying to figure out what will work best for the meal.
>
> Sandy Proctor, a maternal and child nutrition expert, said, it is important to make a meal that is both healthy and creative.
>
> "A good sack lunch is one that has a variety of food from several food groups", Proctor said. It also features food

with a variety of textures, flavours, colours, and even temperatures, when possible.

"The important thing to remember", she said, is that children need to gain *nutritionally* from foods packed in their lunch boxes".

"Healthy foods contain whole grain breads, fruits without added sugar, vegetables, and milk. Within these general guidelines there can be so much variety", she said, "examples can include a peanut butter banana sandwich on whole wheat bread, a whole wheat tortilla turkey wrap that includes some of the veggies in the sandwich.

"Baked chips and salsa can add a lot of flavour— and a serving of vegetables, too. I try to make sack lunches very simple to eat, keeping fuss and mess to a minimum", Proctor said. "While an apple pie might work for a sack lunch, I would probably opt for an apple or even a serving of apple sauce".

What has been said for packing school lunches also holds true for the school cafeteria. *Adequate nutrition* is needed in order that the student receives the energy necessary to do school work in a satisfying way. Students need to be in good health to engage in ongoing activities, wholeheartedly. They need to achieve objectives of instruction by participating in a variety of learning opportunities. Mandated as well as school objectives need to be achieved. Learning opportunities need to be challenging to develop optimal learner achievement. Motivation, effort, and efficacy on the part of the student are necessary. Proper nutrition is needed to assist in making for healthy and energetic students. A desire to learn and achieve must be in the offing. How well the student does in school may make for success or lack thereof in the future. Thus, nutritional needs must be met.

The late A.H. Maslow (1954), listed basic needs which students possess as they make progress in school. The first listed are physiological needs. Adequate food, clothing, and shelter are truly basics and must be met before higher levels of needs come into being such as gaining relevant subject matter and different skills/methods to use in learning.

When supervising university student teachers in the public schools, I experienced seniors in one high school, in a city of about 3000 people, who walked out collectively from the lunchroom to show disapproval of the lunches being served. The superintendent of schools and the high school principal met with the students to try to resolve the problem. The seniors complained about the following:

- the food was cold,
- the lunchroom was not cleaned properly,
- variety in the kinds of foods served was lacking.

Foods being served met state/federal nutrition needs, but there were other kinds of deficiencies. School lunches are too be hot/warm, but these were cold. Unclean facilities should not be tolerated. This can make for air borne bacteria. Then too, no one likes the same kinds of foods to be served again and again. The superintendent and school principal met with the cafeteria workers and with the custodians to discuss the complaints presented by the high school seniors. They agreed to eat in the school lunchroom once a week to supervise the agreed upon changes. This seemingly ended the justified complaints. Sometimes, it takes the time and attention of school administrators to make for needed changes in the school lunchroom.

As early as 1917, The National Education Association (NEA) came out with the Seven Cardinal Principles of Education. The first objective listed in concept form was "health". Good nutrition is involved here when individuals' are to be healthy persons in school. Quality mental health, too, was salient in the Seven Cardinal Principles of Education. Pupils need to be relatively free of tension, anxiety, and fear. Feelings of safety need to abound in school and in society. Children who are abused will definitely not do well in school. Rather, they must be accepted, loved, and assisted to realize optimum achievement. Active children participate in physical education activities, supervised properly to assist in making for well rounded individuals (See Biswal, 2007).

The whole child is involved in learning. To do well academically and to attain objectives of instruction, the pupil needs to be accepted as a human being having much worth. This means that physiological needs must be met consisting of proper nutrition, clothing, and shelter. Freedom from unsafe conditions need to be present including abuse in its diverse forms. Pupils should be assisted to develop feelings of belonging to groups in school and in society. Within the framework of belongingness, the learner needs to feel that he/she can make salient contributions and thus have esteem needs met (Maslow, 1954).

REFERENCES

Biswal, Gopal Charan (2007), "Physical and vital Education", *Edutracks*, 6 (9), 22, 23, 26. The writer is on the Editorial Board of Edutracks which is published in India.

Ediger, Marlow, and D. Bhaskara Rao (2007), *Administration of Schools*. New Delhi, India: Discovery Publishing House. 1-8.

Hoy, Wayne, and Cecil G. Miskel (2005), *Educational Administration*. Seventh Edition. Boston: McGraw-Hill, Chapter One.

Hutson, Kaylea (2007), "What's for Lunch? Fixing Meals A Student' Will Eat", *Kirksville, Missouri, Daily Express*, September 14, page two.

Maslow, A.H. (1954), *Motivation and Personality*. New York: Harper and Row.

14

SPEAKING ACTIVITIES AND STUDENTS IN SCHOOLS

Oral communication is used frequently in the four language arts areas—reading, writing, listening, and speaking—in school and in society. This manuscript will focus upon oral communication or speaking experiences for pupils. Teachers need to plan the scope and sequence of speaking experiences. Scope emphasizes the breadth of oral communication experiences whereas sequence stresses the order of these activities. A planned program of oral communication experiences in the school curriculum needs to be in evidence. Adequate time must be given to the oral communication curriculum. Clarity of expression must be in the offing to communicate effectively with others.

DIVERSITY IN ORAL COMMUNICATION ACTIVITIES

A variety of speaking activities must be stressed so that quality communication may be practiced. The speaker has the responsibility to communicate ideas accurately to listeners. Proper stress, pitch, juncture, and intonation need to be inherent in the speaking process.

Discussing what has been read in an ongoing lesson/unit of study provides excellent opportunities to practice oral communication skills. The discussion may occur in a large group setting or within a committee of learners. There are definite criteria which need to be followed in the discussion. Participants need to stay on the topic. Straying from the topic discussed might well lead to disorganized thinking. Rude behaviours needs to be eliminated. With rude behaviour belittling occurs and selected pupils may then not participate. All should have ample opportunities to participate actively in a discussion without fear of retribution for ideas presented. Ideas should circulate within a group and receive attention for inherent quality. Content which is vague and lacks clarity must be modified in order to be meaningful. The teacher may model in a think aloud on working effectively in a group discussion setting. Courtesy and manners must be a part of the think aloud.

Critical and creative thinking should be practiced within any oral communication activity.

Second, pupils may be involved in a brain storming experience. Generating ideas is salient in brain storming. Thus, in a literature selection, pupils may generate ideas on the kind of character represented in a short story. Each contribution needs to be recorded on the chalkboard so that duplication of ideas is not present. The more ideas presented, the better. Brainstorming also may be energized in the following parts of the short story:

- setting of story
- plot or what happened in the reading selection
- recurring theme or underlying message presented

- alternate points of view in the story
- point of view
- satire to be added in brain storming (Ediger and Rao, 2007a).

Third, readers theater is a good oral communication activity, providing pupils are ready for participating. Here, pupils may workout speaking parts from a narrative library book. An interesting story may then be rewritten of divided into appropriate parts. The parts chosen need to make for a meaningful whole. Pupils may then select who is to read aloud each part to an audience. Planning co-operatively is an important part of reader's theater. Practice is necessary to read aloud with enthusiasm and meaningfully. Each participant may sit in a chair in front of the audience. Neighbouring classrooms may be invited to hear the reader's theater presentation. Or, pupils may be invited to visit other classrooms for the reader's theater presentation (Ediger and Rao, 2007b).

Commercially developed reader's theater may also be purchased. Reader's theater assists pupils to practice quality read alouds. Feelings of self-confidence might well be developed when performing in front of others. Oral communication in different forms can make for rich learner experiences. Neuman (2006) lists the following features of effective content and language rich experiences:

- Time, materials, and resources that actively help students build language and conceptual knowledge
- A supportive learning environment in which students have access to a wide variety of print resources
- Experiences that help students connect new learnings to what they already know and can do

- Opportunities for sustained indepth learning
- High levels of teacher interaction to assist and guide student's learning.

Thus, background knowledge is needed together with ongoing experiences to achieve well in the language arts. Quality oral communication depends upon a wealth of concepts and generalizations used in speaking, including reader's theater.

Fourth, impromptu speaking might be challenging to many learners. Here, the pupil may select a topic, from a given list, and provide a related oral report within a time limit such as five minutes. The pupil then brings to bear background information to present the talk. It takes rather quick thinking to access information which will shed light on the topic. There are time limits in getting the oral presentation together. Organization is important in impromptu speaking. When readiness exists, this might well be an exciting way to give a talk to the class. Again, this speaking activity needs to be done in an atmosphere of respect which encourages oral communication experiences. As is true of all speaking experiences, impromptu speaking integrates oral communication with reading, writing, listening and speaking.

Although this manuscript deals with oral communication through rich experiences in language. There are additional means of communication such as through the arts. Certainly, individuals, for example, communicate' effectively through music. The author plays the baritone horn, intermittently since 1940. However since 1980, he practices each day for approximately 30 minutes for enjoyment and enrichment. In high school music contests, the author received highly superior ratings at district music festivals. There is considerable joy in playing different numbers at church and civic events, and it does communicate well to the self as well as toward others. Feller and Gibbs- Griffith wrote the following in teaching content through the arts:

> In 2005-06, our students demonstrated a 47% drop in discipline referrals and an incredible 67% drop in out of school suspensions. We have seen improvements in students' communication skills, team building skills, empathy, and pride. Verbal attacks against other students' character has been replaced by positive statements and encouraging remarks. Classes have fewer disruptions; students are on task, engaged, and excited about learning. Music is no longer a class to just memorize facts about dead composers; it has become an attitude-altering place where students learn more than how to playa drum—they learn how to live.

The program directs student energy toward musical accomplishment, team work and service toward others. Additional goals included to engage students, improve achievement and morale, and teach important life skills. The latter three objectives, in particular, are salient in any curriculum area as well as in the societal arena. However team work and service toward others are also important; music activities, many times, can be integrated into the curriculum within ongoing units of study. Oral communication will be involved, for example, when students are actively participating in teaching and learning situations.

Sixth, creative dramatics in oral communication are important. Here, pupils with teacher guidance may take a familiar, just completed narrative story and develop it into a related dramatization. Students with teacher guidance select who will take specific roles in the creative dramatics presentation. Memorization of parts is not advocated since creativity is inherent in the dramatization. Background scenery is not needed unless it is necessary for a presentation, such as an imaginary bridge in "The Three Billy Goats Gruff". Otherwise spontaneity is encouraged in the creative dramatics presentation. Novelty and uniqueness need to be emphasized.

Seventh, story telling is salient not only in the school curriculum but it also is stressed when people get together in society. Students, here, may tell a story based on what was read such as in a fable, tall tale, legend, myth, or fairy tale. The story may also be created by the pupil. The learner needs to have the story well in mind and yet be flexible in its telling orally. Several of my student teachers whom I supervised in the public schools emphasized Goldilocks and the three Bears in their presentations for story telling. Most children enjoy the art of story telling.

In closing, there are a plethora of oral communication activities available for children. The teacher needs to be on the lookout for innovative, creative ways of using language orally. Reading, along with other methods of securing information, provide springboards for speaking activities. What is spoken can also be written down using a variety of purposes. Oral use of language assists students to engage in active listening. Being a good listener is salient in school as well as in the societal arena.

REFERENCES

Ediger, Marlow, and D. Bhaskara Rao (2007a), *Reading Curriculum and Instruction*. New Delhi, India: Discovery Publishing House, 188-192.

Ediger, Marlow, and D. Bhaskara Rao (2007b), *Curriculum of School Subjects*. New Delhi, India: Discovery Publishing House, 153-159.

Feller, Thomas R., Jr. and Brian Gibbs-Griffith, "Teaching Content Through the Arts", *Educational Leadership*, 68 (8), 48-49.

Neuman, Susan B. (2006), "N is for Nonsensical", *Educational Leadership*, 64(2), 31.

15

READING WORDLESS BOOKS AND STUDENTS IN SCHOOLS

Wordless, illustrated picture books definitely have their role in the total reading program. There are excellent wordless library books which are suitable for reading on different achievement levels in reading. This is especially true for the young child who is not ready to read abstract words and for older children who are struggling in learning to read. When should the wordless reading program be emphasized?

WORDLESS LIBRARY BOOKS

The infant, when ready, may look at the large illustrations in selected wordless books when seated on the parentis lap. The wordless book needs to be carefully selected to actively engage the infant. The attention span will be short and the parent should not force the child to attend, but rather the interests of the infant should propel attention. Engaging the infant in this activity will assist in generating background information for reading. Learning is sequential and with involved interest, the infant will be aided in cumulative learnings. Then too, a personal relationship is developed between parent and child.

In the pre-school years, ages three and four, learners begin to ask questions as they become curious about the illustrations. They may even begin to tell stories about the pictures. Favourite books will be looked again and again. It is good to have the child choose which books to look at sequentially.

The attention span has lengthened as the pre-school child begins to tell about pictures in a book. At a young age, children may enjoy reading content from illustrations. They learn to love library books as well as appreciate the fascinating illustrations therein. The illustrations tell a story. The child is learning that reading is done in a left to right manner and the front of the book is the starting point. There are specific pictures which will fascinate the child and he/she will point out these features. The adult, too, may point out interesting parts of a picture (Ediger and Rao, 2004).

Reading and interpreting wordless books might well stress higher levels of cognition on the developmental level of the child. Re-reading a wordless book generates familiarity of the contents and then encourages the learner to review what has been learned. With re-reading, the child may think of new interpretations and ideas. The excitement of re-reading illustrations which fascinate the learner is truly a rich experience. The young child may select what is to be reread. Quickly, young children reveal their favourite books. They will point to an illustration excitedly and tell what is on the ensuing page when re-reading occurs. Interest is a powerful factor in learning.

Children always attempt to attach meaning to wordless books. They try to make sense out of pictures and taking time to talk about what the child is interested in pays off well for the child in attaching meaning to what is being read. The illustrations vary in level of difficulty. It may take more time to decipher the meaning of an illustration in a particular book as compared to others. Activating the child's prior knowledge is always significant in understanding what is being viewed (Heller, December/January, 2006-2007).

It is good for the child to relate wordless books being viewed. Knowledge perceived to be related is less likely to be forgotten as compared to that which is unrelated. It is the learner who needs assistance in do the relating. Relating ideas aids in retention of learnings.

The perspectives of illustration will vary from a close up scene as compared to one further away. Children may become fascinated with this variation.

PICTURE BOOKS WITH LARGE PRINT

Large illustrations with print books may be used as wordless books with young children in the pre-school/ kindergarten years as well as the primary grade levels. Interest in printed words will start for selected pupils who are ready on the kindergarten level. It is always important to notice if readiness factors are there for beginning reading of words. The illustrations assist a pupil in reading the related words and sentences. Thus, if a child can not identify a word correctly, he/she may look at the related picture in the book to secure needed clues. Picture clues are heavy in library books for young children. They are salient to use in word recognition. Then too, using picture clues assists in attaching meaning to what is being read. Background information for the ensuing words and sentences to be read help learners in attaching meaning to ongoing reading experiences. Included in the background information are vocabulary terms for pupil acquisition. Large illustrations certainly can aid in future reading achievement as well as developing readiness for the actual reading of abstract words, phrases, and sentences.

Word play may be stressed when pupils are ready. Thus, a pupil may provide a word which rhymes with the pictured "man" or "pet". Words may be noted which begin alike. How much of word play to emphasize will depend upon readiness factors exhibited by the learner (See Tiedt, 1982).

Pictures need to be studied by pupils on all grade levels. They provide opportunities for growth in developing knowledge and skills in and of themselves. The writer well remembers a seventh grade pupil he taught in a small rural school in the early 1950s who read very immaturely, but had a fairly good knowledge of history due to interests possessed in this area. The student looked at illustrations in the only set of encyclopedias located in the classroom. He spent hours, literally, during the school year browsing through these encyclopedias, repeatedly.

Pictures may be used for discussion purposes in describing what exists in the illustration as well as for relating different illustrations. If pictures are sequentially arranged, pupils can be asked to predict what will happen next when viewing an illustration. There can certainly be diverse predictions which might well emphasize creative thinking.

When discussing illustrations in context with the related printed script, pupils may make predictions and then check each prediction with what actually transpires in the story. Each contribution must be respected so that feelings of freedom exist for participating.

From wordless picture books, pupil readiness may be directed toward developing an experience chart. Thus, pupils may share pictures viewed for one or more books and present ideas for the experience chart. The pupils state what they desire to go into the chart. Each sentence is copied on the chalk board by the teacher. Learners may then see talk written down. What is said aloud is then encoded. When the experience chart has been completed, the teacher points to each word which he/she reads aloud. Pupils have opportunities to observe the teacher decoding the contents through oral reading. The teacher observes children as he/she reads aloud to see if they are following the script. Then the children in class read aloud together with the teacher as the latter points to sequential words in the chart. The contents may be re-read with teacher guidance to develop pupil proficiency in word recognition. A basic sight vocabulary should be an end result for learners. Additional experience charts may be developed from other illustrations. These experience charts may be filed and reused later, as the need arises. Many times, pupils like to re-read subject matter. This makes for feelings of security and enjoyment.

DEVELOPING READINESS FOR READING FROM A BIG BOOK

Large library books containing attention securing illustrations may be used for teaching a small group of five to six pupils. It is salient that all can see the illustrations and script clearly. First, the illustrations need to be discussed to develop meaning and activate the intellect for the ensuing reading experience. The teacher then reads aloud the related script with pupils following along as the words are being read. The teacher should point to the words and phrases as the read aloud progresses. Careful observation of learners must be in evidence to determine if they are following along in viewing the printed materials being read orally by the teacher. With the second read aloud, pupils also join in with the teacher. The co-operative endeavour with pupils and the teacher may continue as often as desired. With the big book approach:

- pictures are read, along with the related print
- pupils are reading the entire selection with teacher guidance
- interest in reading ideas is stressed without interruptions from teaching word recognition techniques
- holism is being stressed in the curriculum.

At the end of the reading aloud experience, time may be given to having pupils notice words having the same beginning sound, rhyming words, and words with a long vowel sound, as competencies permit. The teacher adjusts the new learnings in terms of readiness levels for pupils.

The interests of learners need to be promoted as much as possible. Interest in reading is a prime factor in developing good readers. The teacher needs to be enthusiastic about reading and share with pupils what he/she has been reading. Leading motivational discussions dealing with the illustrations as well as with the related script assists pupils to show exhilaration for the act of reading.

Reasons for reading pictures and script are very salient. If pupils are to perceive purpose in reading, they need to accept viable reasons for engaging in the process of improving skills to read smoothly. Different reasons presented to pupils at diverse times might well indeed foster purpose for reading. Showing excitement and enthusiasm for reading by teachers and pupils should be a good motivator for all (See Palincsar and Brown, 1984).

READING IN THE SUBJECT MATTER AREAS

What has been discussed so far, also applies in reading in the content areas. Thus, the big book approach and experience charts may relate directly to science, social studies, and mathematics. There are excellent picture books with related print put out by leading organizations in their academic areas of specialty such as the National Council for the Social Studies (NCSS), The National Council for Teachers of Mathematics (NCTM), The National Science Teachers Association (NSTA), The International Reading Association (IRA), and the National Council Teachers of English (NCTE). These organizations and services provided may be accessed on the internet, including information on publications and listed books for pupils.

Textbooks in each subject matter area in unit teaching contain many useful illustrations. These may provide necessary background information to children when viewed carefully and discussed with pupils in the classroom. The pictures may well activate cognitive background learnings for pupils. The illustrations also assist pupils to relate to themselves, to society, and the natural environment. New vocabulary terms may be introduced through teacher discussions of pictures as well as by writing these terms in neat manuscript style on the chalkboard. Pupils might then become familiar with the new words and recognize them while reading the ensuing content. Phonics learnings may be stressed as necessary. Problems and questions need to be identified by pupils with teacher guidance. Solutions and answers may be found through silent reading. Additional information sources may need to be used for the unsolved/ unanswered (Ediger and Rao, 2000).

Reading information through pictures may be used at all elementary school levels as well as in secondary school. There is much information which may be secured from viewing pictures. Added and modified information comes into being with related printed script. Valuable facts, concepts, and generalizations accrue in this way, leading to inferential, critical and creative thinking.

REFERENCES

Ediger, Marlow, and D. Bhaskara Rao (2004), *Psychology and Curriculum*. New Delhi, India: Discovery Publishing House.

Ediger, Marlow, and D. Bhaskara Rao (2000), *Teaching Reading Successfully*. New Delhi, India: Discovery Publishing House.

Heller, Mary F. (December/January, 2006-2007), "Telling Stories and Talking Facts, First Graders' Engagement in a Nonfiction Book Club". *The Reading Teacher*, 60 (4), 358-369.

Palincsar, A.S., and A.L. Brown (1984), "Reciprocal Teaching of Comprehension Fostering and Comprehension Monitoring Activities", *Cognition and Instruction*, 1, 117-175.

Tiedt, Iris M. (1982), *The Language Arts Handbook*. Englewood Cliffs, New Jersey: Prentice-Hall, Inc.

16

PURPOSEFUL READING AND STUDENTS IN SCHOOLS

Without purpose, there are a lack of reasons for students pursuing objectives of instruction. Objectives of instruction need to be well thought through and possess reasons for their accomplishment. Teachers individually, as well as committees, need to work diligently to define what students need to learn. Professional organizations, too, have long sought after and gleaned relevant ends of instruction. With the many statements of objectives available, it behooves teachers to emphasize purpose in teaching and learning situations. To be sure, not all objectives can be stated prior to instruction. Objectives emerge when students raise questions during a lesson or unit of study and these might well be vital to pursue. Purposeful learning is of utmost importance (Kennedy, 2006).

PURPOSE IN READING

How might teachers teach if purpose in reading is emphasized throughout each lesson/unit of study? When basal readers are being used, the teacher assists students to attach meaning to new words introduced for the ensuing lesson. The purpose for this activity may be stated by the teacher as, "These are new words you will meet in print as you read the new story. This will help you to identify each word, as well as understand their meaning as you read silently". Thus, there is a purpose involved in studying the new words on the chalkboard. Based on the contextual illustrations in the basal, students hypothesize what the contents of the story will be about. The purpose here may be, "Lets see how close our guesses will be on the content of the story to be read". Students are then ready to read the ensuing story. A purpose-driven strategy in reading will also continue after the story has been read with the following:

- lets see how closely we predicted what the story would be about. Here, questions will arise and need to be discussed.
- when we read the story aloud, several missed identifying the following words: science (silent letters), rocks (double consonant), metamorphic (ph letters), erosion (sion letters), sedimentary (tary). It have indicated the trouble spots in identifying these words in parenthesis. "We need to practice pronouncing these words correctly so they may be identified accurately". (Ediger and Rao, 2001).

Individualized reading has several forms. One of these is to encourage children to take library books home to read. Here, the teacher introduces a few books by holding them up for all to see. Students then volunteer to check out selected books for home reading. Stated purposes involve the interesting content each library book has for reading enjoyment. During sharing time in school, students individually may tell of a few interesting things read from home reading.

A second variation of individualization is for a student to read a self-chosen book during Sustained Silently Reading (SSR). The stated purpose here is to enjoy reading and refine skills during a special time set aside for this activity during the school day. Book jackets from new library books as well as teacher comments of fascinating subject matter might well whet learner appetites for selecting and choosing reading materials. Ideas from reading may be made during the current lesson and unit of study as the library book content makes contextual contributions.

A third variation of individualized reading has an extended evaluation session to ascertain student comprehension, skill in word recognition, and fluency in reading progress. Thus, after the learner has completed reading a library book, he/she has a conference with the teacher to evaluate each of the three previously mentioned areas of achievement. Brief records are made of each area of achievement and the ensuing records may be kept for reference in sequential conferences. A conference is then held after the completion of reading a library book. The purpose for conducting sequential conferences may well be stated to notice if achievement has taken place from one time to the next time (Ediger, 2003).

THE BIG BOOK APPROACH

The big book procedure of reading instruction is a holistic approach. Here, the teacher chooses a large book from which fix or síx students may be taught at one time. Each learner must be able to see the contents clearly. The illustrations are discussed first in the big book. This provides background information to children for reading the ensuing contents. The teacher reads the contents aloud the first time while pointing to each word as children follow along. Next, students read the same content aloud' together with the teacher. This procedure may be repeated as often as necessary. Learners then read the content independently while developing a basic sight vocabulary. Meaning is attached to the story at the same time. Students do not need to struggle over the identification of unrecognized words, but may holistically attend to understanding the content.

There are several purposes which the teacher may communicate to students in using the big book in reading:

- First, we will discuss the illustrations in a book which I think you will enjoy.
- I will read aloud the first time so that you do not miss out on content due to difficult to recognize words. Notice each word carefully as I point to it while reading.
- After this, you may read the story to yourself.

It is salient that students understand each purpose while the reading lesson is being introduced and implemented (See Liang and Dole, 2006).

Too frequently, reading teachers make assignments without stating a purpose.

This makes it appear as if the teacher wants children to do certain things in reading without a reason for doing so. Reading lessons then appear to have no purpose. It is purpose that helps motivate students to succeed. The teacher needs to choose a purpose for those needing to do the assignments, not for those who have already experienced success in achieving a given objective. Each purpose or reason should be stated clearly so students understand why an exercise is to be completed. Thus, the following phonic learnings should have a purpose, understandable to students, for those who need assistance:

- identify syllables so that words may be analyzed for identification purposes
- identify onsets and rimes to notice patterns in word recognition
- notice short and long vowel sounds as well as those vowel letters governed by the letter "r".
- notice words which follow the consonant/vowel/consonant/silent "e". pattern. The vowel letter then generally has a long vowel sound. Limitations to this generalization needs to be pointed out to students.
- over-generalizing should be avoided in which words must be learned by sight in reading and in spelling, e.g. through, though, bough, rough, among others.

There are standards which need to be followed in determining which rules students need to learn/follow in reading subject matter. These rules should be inclusive of many phonic generalizations. Thus, the "can" family of words pattern in spelling and reading such as ban, fan, man, pan, among others are consistent. Whereas the rule, "When two vowels go together, the first one does the talking", has too many loop holes including heart, health, hearth, breath, breadth. Second, vowel rules should pertain to relevant learnings, not to one or two cases. Thus, consistency of the rule is salient. Third, there must be a purpose in studying a rule, not memorizing a rule for the sake of doing so. Fourth, the rule needs to be taught meaningfully so it makes sense to the learner. Fifth, too frequently, rules have been taught for the sake of doing so, not for utilitarian reasons. Use needs to be made of what has been learned. Purposeful learning is always important (Duke, 2006).

TECHNOLOGY IN THE READING CURRICULUM

Technology has much to offer in improving reading instruction. There are a plethora of computerized products available which need assessment, prior to purchasing. Again, there needs to be a purpose stated in an interesting manner, in using technology to improve instruction. Will a certain technology assist students in achieving vital objectives in reading? Even with technological use, certain students fail to benefit the way they should.

As assistive technologies have advanced over the years, they have delivered instruction in new ways. But simply improving access and delivery will not necessarily improve instruction. On the contrary, improved learning for all students depends upon the quality of instruction—not on the medium with which it is delivered.

As teachers, we must become more aware of the role technology plays in learning. One main focus as educators who care for youth with learning disabilities to profit from good instruction, technology is not magic; it is simply a tool of education. As with any tool, when used skillfully, it can help achieve spectacular results (Hesselbring and Bausch, 2006).

A good teacher needs to have reasons for emphasizing selected objectives in teaching and learning. It is not because a manual in the basal textbook stresses it as necessary, but rather the teacher identifies specific learnings as being essential in helping individuals progress sequentially in reading. Problems in reading well are specific to the learner. The purpose then is to identify, teach, and remediate the involved difficulty. Continuous progress in reading for each student is a must!

REFERENCES

Duke, Daniel L. (2006), "What We Know and Don't Know Abut Improving Low Performing Schools", *Phi Delta Kappan*, 87 (10), 729- 739.

Ediger, Marlow (2003), "Mentor teachers", *Edutracks*, 2 (9), 9-15. Published in India.

Ediger, Marlow, and D. Bhaskara Rao (2006), *Teaching Reading Successfully*. New Delhi, India: Discovery Publishing House.

Hesselbring, Ted S., and Margaret E. Bausch (2006), "Assistive technologies for Reading", *The Reading Teacher*, 63 (4),72-75.

Kennedy, Mary M. (2006), "From Teacher Quality to Quality Teaching", *Educational Leadership*, 63 (6), 14-19.

Liang, Lauren Aimonette, and Janice A. Dole, (2006), "Help with Teaching Reading Comprehension: Comprehensional Frameworks", *The Reading Teacher*, 59 (8),742-753.

17

PROFESSIONAL DEVELOPMENT OF TEACHERS IN SCHOOLS

Teachers need to grow and develop continuously in the teaching profession. After receiving the bachelor's degree to teach, an inservice education program needs to ensue. Inservice education programs must be broad in scope to encompass that which is necessary for a teacher to pursue. It also must follow sequentially in activities to provide meaningful experiences. Purpose, also, in pursuing each activity needs to be in the offing. Thus, there are reasons for the pursuit of each activity. Inservice education then is not done for the sake of doing so, but rather to fulfill a reason and that reason being to improve instruction.

PURPOSEFUL INSERVICE ACTIVITIES

Self-evaluation is very important in determining areas of inservice growth. One area of growth necessary to improve instruction is computer literacy and proficiency in teaching. There are salient objectives which students need to achieve in working with computers. To achieve vital objectives of instruction, students needs assistance in computer efficiency. The teacher may discover that there are personal needs in becoming increasingly proficient in assisting students with computer activities. Self-evaluation then indicates needs. A workshop may need to be held or a supervisor might well provide the necessary assistance. The point is that the teacher find the help needed to become a better teacher when students need computer assistance in ongoing learning activities (See, Van Horn, 2006).

A second area of growth teachers need to improve teaching proficiency is in subject matter knowledge. Within the frame-work of teaching, the teacher may well notice a deficiency in teaching selected facts, concepts, and generalizations. Here, the teacher may need to do professional reading of that which he/she is lacking. The teacher might wish to take a course online or on a university campus to increase knowledge which is useful for teaching. There are many avenues open to develop well in professional knowledge to improve the curriculum. Subject matter knowledge needs to be updated to remain current in the field. A schedule of daily reading will help to remain current in subject matter knowledge (Ediger and Rao, 2005).

Methods of teaching must be used which assist students to achieve as optimally as possible. Thus, reading journal articles dealing with teaching methodology of the area of specialization the teacher is in, needs to receive much attention. Subject matter knowledge is important, but equally so are ways of imparting knowledge to learners. Thus, a social studies teacher, for example, needs to use updated methods of instruction, including:

- inductive and deductive methods.

- problem solving procedures.
- project methodology and activities.
- multi-media techniques
- print materials such as basals, a carefully chosen textbook, as well as library books (See, Hasselbring and Bausch, 2006).

Methodology used needs to assist students to achieve viable objectives of instruction. Resources are there for students to use in ongoing lessons and units of study. Educational psychology has recommendations for curriculum improvement including:

- interesting activities need to be chosen which guide learners to attain objectives.
- students need to perceive purpose or reasons for participating in ongoing experiences.
- meaning must be attached to ongoing lessons/units of study.
- active involvement in learning needs to be fostered.
- co-operative learning must be stressed to assist students in social development.
- individual talents and abilities must be enhanced (Gardner, 1993).

Teachers must make sure that the concepts being studied and the knowledge and skills required to deal successful with them are compatible with student's level of intellectual, physical, social, and emotional development. Teachers must avoid attempting to teach concepts that are obviously too complex for their students or for which students have not mastered necessary prerequisite skills. Instead, teachers must constantly analyze their students' abilities and determine what they are capable of handling and learning successfully.

If it becomes apparent that concepts to be studied require higher levels of intellectual development than students possess, teachers should either postpone teaching the concepts or should not teach them at all (Brown, 2003).

The learning environment must be conducive to helping students achieve. A friendly, business like atmosphere needs to prevail. Here, students are busy getting and using materials to achieve lesson and unit goals of instruction. It is good if schools study the environment under which students learn to ascertain if it is of high quality. An attitude of goodwill and eagerness to assist students, teachers, school administrators, and support personnel should be in the offing. A positive, caring environment helps students to achieve more optimally, including:

- acceptable noise levels, temperature readings, and setting arrangements.
- choices as to what to learn, and as well as conformity vs. non-comformity behaviour settings.
- individual endeavours vs collective learning opportunities.
- collegial relations vs a more structured learning environment.
- using visual/auditory, and or kinesthetic ways of learning.
- moving around in the classroom to engage in learning vs. sitting still to achieve more optimally.
- eating vs non-eating while doing homework.
- being an analytical learner in a step by step sequence vs. holistic approaches in achieving (Searson and Dunn, 2001).

Goodwill needs to expand to the community level. Parents, in particular, need to feel welcome to express needs of their children. Parent/teacher co-operation is necessary for the benefit of the student. Schools exist for students, but the total educational enterprise must be supported for excellence in education to accrue.

REFERENCES

Brown, David M. (2003), "Learner Centered Conditions that Ensure Student's Success in Learning", *Education*, 124 (1), 99 -104.

Ediger, Marlow, and D. Bhaskara Rao (2005), *Quality School Education*. New Delhi, India: Discovery Publishing House.

Gardner, Howard (1993), *Multiple Intelligences: Theory into Practice*. New York: Basic Books.

Hasselbring, and Bausch (2006), "Assistive Technologies for Reading", *Educational Leadership*, 63 (4), 72-75.

Searson, Robert, and Rita Dunn (2001), "The Learning Style Teaching Model", *Science and Children*, 38 (5), 22-36.

Van Horn, Royal (2006), "Technology", *Phi Delta Kappan*, 87 (10), 727-792.

18

TUTORING STUDENTS TO ACHIEVE IN SCHOOLS

Tutoring has always been a salient part of education and schooling. When attending elementary school, 1934-1942, selected pupils were tutored after school, free, with no extra salary for teachers. It was then considered customary, evidently, for teachers to tutor those needing extra assistance.

Presently, moneys are available for tutoring pupils who qualify under federal guidelines. Specially approved tutors then are available to help pupils. What should be the qualifications for tutoring pupils?

QUALIFICATIONS FOR TUTORS

Tutors need to be accepting of others, especially pupils of school age. A warm, caring relationship needs to be in the offing. The tutor needs to be knowledgeable pertaining to the curriculum areas being tutored. If tutoring in the area of reading instruction, the tutor must specialize in different areas of assisting pupils to read. For instance, There are many areas of reading/diagnosis which need consideration in tutoring pupils:

- consistently spelled words
- partial consistency sound/symbol relationship
- words classified as being spelled inconsistently
- vowels (short, long, and those governed by the "r" ending sound
- words with silent letters
- consonant/vowel/consonant/silent "e" pattern, within a word
- consonant/vowel/consonant pattern of words
- consonant and vowel digraphs
- diphthongs
- onset and rimes as well as short words contained in long words (Ediger and Rao, 2007, pp. 5 and 6).

Being able to diagnose and remedy pupil reading problems is salient. Both holism and phonic methods should be used. It is important, too, to consider the interests of the pupil when developing a curriculum for the tutee. Interest is a powerful factor in learning.

The tutor needs to begin tutoring in a reader in which the pupil is able to pronounce approximately ninety five per-cent of the words correctly and answer seventy five per-cent of the related comprehension questions correctly. These are not absolute figures, but do present a guideline for tutoring reading. Thus, the tutor needs to select at random 100 running words and have the tutee read the contents aloud. The kinds of errors in reading aloud may be noticed and recorded. Questions may then be asked of the tutee to evaluate reading comprehension on the same selection.

The above procedure provides a basis for determining the present reading level of the involved pupil. For the same new sequential selection, the teacher may read aloud with the pupil following along in his reader. Next, the pupil and the teacher together may read the same selection, followed by the read aloud by the pupil. If the pupil does well, he/she might read aloud by the self in the ensuing selection, otherwise the same original procedure may be used. Holism is used when the learner reads together with the teacher or by the self to comprehend ideas (Gunning, 2000).

Errors made by the pupil in reading should be recorded by the tutor and dated. If a phonics error, the tutor may assist in helping the child associate symbol (grapheme) with sound (phoneme). If the unidentified words are non-phonetic, they may then be printed on three by five inch cards and learned as sight words. Practice in identifying each word assists the pupil to master its identification. Reinforcement theory may be used here in that an inexpensive reward may be given for achievement and progress in word recognition. Additional pupil errors to be recorded include the following:

- skipping words which are essential for comprehension
- repeating words, phrases, and sentences which already have been read correctly. There are advocates who believe that pupils who comprehend well do repeat selected words, phrases, and sentences to evaluate their individual personal comprehension of ideas read.
- substituting words which hinder in accurate reading
- leaning upon background knowledge in place of reading what the print states
- adding unnecessary commas, periods, and question marks
- omitting punctuation marks (Ediger, 1997).

Based on diagnosis of the above types of errors made by pupils, a better plan of tutoring may be in the offing. It is salient to be able to read fluently with good comprehension in order for pupils to become proficient in reading. Thus, quality objectives stressing knowledge ends need to be emphasized such as knowledge of phonics, syllabication, punctuation, and comprehension of subject matter read. These may be taught in context or in isolation as needed, but the result should stress holism in pupils securing ideas. Skills objectives emphasize pupils using knowledge acquired in diverse reading situations such as using phonetic principles in word recognition and in reading comprehension. Attitudinal objectives stress the feeling dimension whereby pupils have positive attitudes toward reading endeavours.

METHODS IN THE TEACHING OF READING

There are a plethora of methodologies which may be used in helping tutees to improve in the area of reading. When focusing upon background information, the tutor may scaffold ideas for reading. Thus, a student might not understand the background of a story, but the teacher through questioning guides the tutee to develop vital concepts and generalizations. The ordered questions lead the pupil to understanding relevant background information. The chances are the tutee will then better understand the story contents. Through scaffolding, the student might well attach meaning to what previously was too complex. For the tutor, it is interesting to observe how, with ordered experiences, the student can achieve what otherwise was too complex.

Questioning the author (QtA) has four basic ideas to be used as guidelines in comprehension:

- viewing the text as a fallible product written by fallible authors
- dealing with the text through questions that are directed toward making sense out of it
- questions as students are reading
- encouraging student collaboration in the construction of meaning (McKeown *et al.*, 1993).

Questioning the author (QtA) involves an open mind of the tutee to raise questions in which vagueness exists pertaining to what an author had written. The inquiries raised, no doubt, will lead to higher levels of cognition, such as critical thinking. The tutee will need to think of possibilities in interpretation of an author's writing. If more than one pupil is being tutored, they may discuss possibilities in making sense of subject matter content. Too frequently, pupils interpret literally that which was written, and yet there are diverse possibilities in inquiry approaches in meaningful reading. Pupils then must interact with the text as active learners, not passive recipients of knowledge.

A second approach might well emphasizes Reciprocal Teaching. Here, the teacher assists the pupil to view and discuss the pictures in a reader and then predict what will transpire in the story. The contents are read and ideas therefrom summarized. Questions are then raised pertaining to the summary. Information gathered is summarized (Palincsar and Brown, 1984). Thus pupils carefully observe the illustrations in content to be read. This provides background information and readiness for the ensuing reading activity. The pupil then engages in reading followed by developing conclusions pertaining to ideas gleaned. Critical thinking might then arise involving the conclusions gained. The QtA and reciprocal reading may be used by one or a small group of pupils in tutoring. To truly comprehend well, pupils need to extend their thinking of subject matter read. Quality comprehension is important for pupils. A major focal point is for learners to understand subject matter read.

A third approach may stress a question/answer securing procedure. Here, the tutee is guided by the tutor to ask questions pertaining to the illustrations at the beginning of the story. Each question needs to be recorded for reference as the act of reading proceeds. The tutee might then read to secure information for one or more of these questions. Possible answers need to be discussed. A thinking situation arises when the learner attempts to match the answer with the question.

A fourth procedure involves the pupil telling what has been read. The story contents need to be told sequentially. The attitudinal dimension of the story teller needs to be assessed such as in:

- enthusiasm of the tutee
- desired accuracy of story telling
- clarity in the presentation of ideas
- wanting to engage in future story telling activities
- enjoyment of the learning opportunity.

Improving reading comprehension and quality of the tutee is the major objective of each comprehension activity (Burns *et al*. 1996).

EVALUATION OF TUTEE ACHIEVEMENT

The tutor needs to evaluate rather continuously how well the tutee is achieving in reading. Tutor observation of the child's progress must be ongoing. Thus, the tutor needs to observe if the tutee is improving in using word recognition techniques. When using diverse word recognition techniques, the pupil should be improving in reading fluency. Then too, the pupil is achieving in comprehension of content. He/she is able to retell the story read more proficiently and with confidence. Then too, the tutee reveals increased ability to answer questions about subject matter read. The tutor notices attitudes such as increased motivation in reading as well as the tutee selecting books to read on his/her own volition.

The pupil should reveal positive attitudes, more so than formerly, in reading narrative, informational, as well as creative literature as in poetry.

The tutor needs to appraise the self when using improved methods of instruction to guide comprehension in reading. This might well indicate the need to:

- engage student attention for the ongoing experience
- provide interesting activities in reading instruction
- assist students to attach meaning to each objective to be attained
- establish student purpose for reading
- provide for individual differences in the classroom.

Students need to keep journals pertaining to what was experienced in reading. Journaling, here, might emphasize students saying orally what has transcribed with the tutor recording ideas presented. It might include questions a pupil has pertaining to the reading selection covered. Also, entries may include impressions of about subject matter read. Co-operative journaling may be emphasized with other tutees and with the tutor in responding to each other's questions and entries. Students should have opportunities to reflect upon content read. Teaching of reading truly becomes a problem solving activity in that answers need to be sought for student inability to achieve in reading (Ediger and Rao, p. 198).

REFERENCES

Burns, Paul C. *et al.* (1996), *Teaching Reading in Today's Elementary School.* Boston: Houghton Mifflin Company.

Ediger, Marlow (1997), *Teaching Reading and the Language Arts in the Elementary School.* Kirksville, Missouri: Simpson Publishing Company.

Ediger, Marlow, and D. Bhaskara Rao (2007), *Reading Curriculum and Instruction.* New Delhi, India: Discovery Publishing House.

Gunning, Thomas G. (2000), *Creating Literacy Instruction for all Children.* Boston: Allyn and Bacon, Inc. Chapter Twelve.

McKeown, M.G. *et al.* 1993), "Grappling with Text Ideas: Questioning the Author", *The Reading Teacher*, 46, 560-566.

Palincsar, A.S., and A.L. Brown (1984), "Reciprocal Teaching of Fostering Comprehension and Comprehension Monitoring Activities", *Cognition and Instruction*, 1, 117-175.

19

PHILOSOPHY OF TESTING, MEASUREMENT AND EVALUATION IN SCHOOLS

There certainly are diverse philosophies involving testing, measuring, and evaluation. Teachers, supervisors, and administrators need to be highly knowledgeable about each approach. The best and most accurate procedure needs to be found to evaluate learner achievement. Information pertaining to each pupil's achievement is needed in order to plan the curriculum more effectively.

HOW SHOULD PUPIL ACHIEVEMENT BE EVALUATED?

Mandated testing emphasizes using standardized tests whereby each student on a grade level takes the same test. The directions for test administration are the same and generally multiple choice test items are used which are the same for each age/grade level of pupils. These tests have been pilot tested to establish appropriate validity and reliability. From the pilot study, norms have been developed.

A pupil's test results from taking the standardized test is compared with that of the norm group to reveal percentile rank or grade equivalent. Numerical, precise scores are then provided as a result of machine scoring.

Mandated tests are given on selected grade levels to indicate passing or failing for a pupil. A school is then held accountable for learner achievement. Basic ideas to support mandated testing include the following:

- measurability is involved in ascertaining pupil progress
- precision in testing procedures are involved
- teachers are held responsible to assist learner's achieving at an acceptable level (Ediger and Rao, 2002).

Toward the opposite end of the continuum, constructionism as a philosophy of education is emphasized. Here, the thinking of proponents stresses the following:

- What is salient to learn is not measurable
- Students need to be more in control of their education, not measurement specialists
- Objectives for student achievement are rather open ended
- Evaluation of learner progress is somewhat subjective
- Self-evaluation is also salient in assessment (Ediger, 2006).

A sample of pupil daily products may be an inherent part of evaluation in a constructivist philosophy of education. Thus, a digital or traditional portfolio might well be developed containing a random sampling of student work including poems, expository/narrative writings, and book reports.

Additional items may include art work, digital pictures of construction projects related directly to an ongoing unit of study, and recordings of oral presentations, as well as committee endeavours, among others.

TEACHER WRITTEN TESTS

Teacher written and administered tests have considerable merit in determining pupil achievement. Each test item must be clearly written to avoid misinterpretations. Multiple choice and essay test items written with the use of appropriate testing and measurement criteria, in particular, may add increased sophistication in test writing. There should be a stem and four plausible distractors of approximate equal length, one of which is clearly correct in the writing of multiple choice test items. The stem must be grammatically correct with each of the responses. No clues should be given as to which is the correct response. If scored by hand, a scoring key for the multiple choice test items needs to be written out prior to checking each student's results. Computerized scoring, although not infallible and if available, should be used to avoid errors in checking the results. Popham (2007), wrote:

> Computers are becoming smarter about scoring students' tests. Today's electronic scoring devices can ingest a flock of students' test answers—some selected responses and some generated responses—and then both score and analyze the very devil out of them. Finally, like the electronic elves they are, computers can chum out a galaxy of score reports for educators, students, parents, and the public.

A rubric may also be developed and used to make for increased objectivity in assessing essay tests. Spelling, grammar, and the mechanics of writing should be evaluated separately from subject matter content in the essay. A five point scale is generally used with each of the five listing what is expected to meet that criterion.

Relevant, factual information might well be assessed through the use of matching test items and completion responses. With matching tests, there need to be two vertical columns with more items in one column as compared to the other so that the process of elimination cannot be used exclusively when matching the two columns. With completion tests, there needs to be enough information given so that students know which information is needed in the blank space. A student would not know the information needed in the following completion test item:—and—are important.

True/false tests are good to use if the student is asked to correct what is incorrect in a false test item. This tends to minimize guessing on whether a test item is true or false. Half the test items should be true and half false. Otherwise if a student merely guesses, for example, that all are "true", and the test would be biased toward the items being "true", then he/she would receive a much higher score than if the exact number of true and false items were the same (See Burton, 2005).

To develop a variety of valid and reliable test items to ascertain learner progress in any curriculum area, the teacher needs to consult university textbooks and journal articles on writing high quality test items. Teacher leadership and school administrative encouragement might well be necessary to assist other teachers in writing quality test items. This may be done with using the following procedures:

- mentoring other teachers in studying and writing quality test items

- conducting a workshop in developing appropriate tests to measure learner progress
- writing and sending a series of newsletters on ways to improve testing and measuring
- meeting with small groups of teachers to motivate in the development of quality tests
- assisting individual teachers pertaining to problematic situations in testing
- developing a professional library with books and periodical articles on improving test item writing
- interpreting formative and summative evaluations.

Knowledgeable teachers need assistance to become change agents and catalysts to help in curriculum improvement. Testing and measuring might well be a curriculum area to work toward to desirable change. Why? There is much testing going on in the public schools at the present time. School personnel must understand how standardized tests are written and developed. They need to attach meaning to concepts such as item analysis, pilot studies, measures of central tendency, standardized scores, standard deviation, quartile deviation, standard error of the mean, experimental studies, and correlational studies, among others.

Additional means of evaluating pupil achievement include teacher observation. This is an excellent approach to use in evaluating student progress. With quality criteria to use in making observations, the teacher may obtain necessary information in assisting students to make continuous progress. The following observations may be made:

- time on task of each student
- politeness and caring behaviour of individual students

- co-operation among students when working on projects
- difficulties and problems faced in learning
- a study of remedial procedures in assisting learners to make for continuous progress
- scaffolding learnings for higher achievement (See Opitz and Ford, 2006).

What is observed may be recorded for future reference. Anecdotal statements may be written at regular intervals. They indicate recorded achievement at specific times. Comparisons may then be made from one dated interval to the next for each pupil. The teacher might then draw improved conclusions on how to assist each pupil to attain more optimally.

Teachers and administrators need to study indepth and evaluate diverse procedures in the evaluation of student achievement. Which approach or approaches appear to do the best job of assessment? Research methodology should be used to the best possible in making these kinds of decisions. Even though there may be mandated evaluation procedures, there still is room for new, innovative procedures to ascertain learner achievement and progress.

REFERENCES

Burton, Kimberly Smith (2005), "Using Student Peer Evaluations to Evaluate Team Taught Lessons", *Journal of Instructional Psychology*, 32 (2),136-138.

Ediger, Marlow, and D. Bhaskara Rao (2002), *Philosophy and Curriculum*. New Delhi, India: Discovery Publishing House.

Ediger, Marlow (2006), ''Testing Versus Portfolios to Assess Achievement", *Oklahoma ASCD Journal*, 13(1), 31-32.

Opitz, Michael E, and Michael P. Ford (2006), "Assessment Can Be Friendly", *The Reading Teacher*, 59(8), 814-816.

Popham, W. James (2007), "Grain Size: The Unresolved Riddle", *Educational Leadership*, 64(8), 80.

20

USING MODELS TO IMPROVE STUDENT ACHIEVEMENT IN SCHOOLS

Selected educators point to model schools as examples to emulate. These schools have been written about in leading educational journals and they are praised for their progress. Perhaps, researchers have shown, through statistical analysis, quality student achievement. Recommendations may then be made to emulate these models. This is one way to stress the importance of using models to improve instruction. However, the local school may not possess the materials of instruction nor the motivation of teachers that the model school has. The local school might be in a low income area with little money on their own to spend on education of students. External validity is then lacking when using the model school to emulate in its entirety. Aspects of the model school might be used to improve the local curriculum such as methods of inservice teacher education. Feasibility is a salient concept to use here in making needed changes locally (Ediger and Rao, 2006).

INNOVATIVE SCHOOLS

In wanting to accept a model school, as a goal to strive toward, selected teachers and a school administrator should visit the school and talk indepth to faculty members. This should result in answering questions which visitors have. Preparation should make for readiness prior to visiting and becoming familiar with the model school. Meaningful deliberations must be in the offing to ascertain which parts of the model school plan may be adopted, if any, on the local level.

Model schools which have had good write ups by well known educators in leading educational journals hold promise for innovations to improve the local school curriculum. Blind acceptance of innovations is not recommended, but they need to be weighed in light of what is possible in improving the curriculum.

A second approach in studying innovations in high achieving schools is to study and view selected charter schools. Charters receive their funding from the local public school district. They have been granted independence from state regulations and red tape which are considered to halt more optimal student achievement. Their major purpose was to develop creative methods of instruction which assist to up learner progress. So far, charters have not been too successful in demonstrating merit. A considerable number lose their status due to corruption and misuse of funds. Then too, the verdict is still out if these kinds of schools are successful in aiding student achievement. A few schools have received a good write up in leading educational journals by reputable educators. These may be selected as schools deemed to be good enough for copying, in part. Actually, no school will be emulated en toto. Situations differ as to what should be modified and adopted. Even a model school will have certain items which need changing as perceived by teachers and administrators in their own schools.

A third procedure might well stress reading of educational literature to determine what expert educators say should be changed to improve learner achievement. The following plans of instruction may be extolled as having much value:

- hands on approaches in student learning including community service
- learner choices, from among alternatives, as to what to learn in the classroom
- field experiences/excursions in life like situations such as testing water quality in a stream or lake
- block of time procedures in teaching and learning
- use of teacher strengths in the instructional arena.

Each innovation studied needs to be analyzed and synthesized to determine which facet(s), if any, should be incorporated into the local curriculum. Poutiatine (2005), reviewed empirical research studies that had been conducted on teacher renewal; these studies indicated that participating teachers:

- articulated a renewed sense of passion for their work
- focused more on creating hospital learning environments for students
- devoted more time to framing good questions and listening to students
- clarified and renewed core beliefs about students and teaching
- committed to taking on leadership roles at their school sites

- deepened their appreciation for collegial relationships.

A fourth procedure in studying model schools is to look at published test results to notice which schools excel according to No Child Left Behind (NCLB). The high test scores might then be used to choose a school to emulate. Results are listed in the media of schools in terms of per cent of students having passed their grade level test as well as schools having met adequate yearly progress (AYP). Measurement philosophy is involved in viewing NCLB test results. Precision is desired here when studying numerical results from students and schools. According to advocates, guesswork is minimized when advocating testing, solely, to ascertain student/school progress.

Databased decision-making is in evidence when a teacher in the classroom or a school administrator makes curricular decisions based on standardized test results. The best schools may then be identified. NCLB choices and decisions are based upon:

- objective evidence, such as from standardized tests
- test scores freed from bias and opinions
- all conditions being the same for test taking be it time limits for completing the ensuing test, directions to be followed, and test items being the same for those taking a grade level test.

Since each state determines their own standards for passing a grade level test and also for the AYP, there is a lack of evidence as to how much students are actually achieving. Uniformity of standards are lacking when comparisons are made among the states. Thus, it is easier to pass to the next grade level in one state as compared to the other. Or, AYP standards are easier to meet in selected states as compared to those having higher standards (Fuller, August 9, 2006).

Studies have not been made on those schools and individuals with high test scores and later success at the work place. Do high test scores then correlate well with quality work done later at the work place?

Fifth, using guidelines to develop a high performing school in terms of learner achievement. A plethora of schoolarly articles in education proclaim the use of guidelines from the psychology of learning in making for effective teaching and learning situations. These tend to be broad guidelines which provide a framework for teaching efficacy. Thus, methods of teaching may stress criteria such as the following to improve the curriculum:

- engage students in ongoing lessons and units of study
- provide interesting learning activities for students to achieve objectives of instruction
- assist students to perceive purpose in learning
- motivate learners to achieve and develop
- provide for individual differences.

By following the above guidelines for inservice education, teachers working in committees may devise related lessons and units of study. Lessons may then be taught in the classroom incorporating these guidelines. Feedback from students provides information to the committee of teachers as to the effectiveness of the incorporated guidelines. Improving the curriculum is a major goal.

Teaches rarely have opportunities to discuss their practice with their peers or critically reflect on their teaching practice. This is especially true for teachers in high poverty schools, which frequently report lower collegial interactions among teachers related to instructional management (Shields *et al.*, 1999).

Sixth, the model schools concept may be developed through the use of action research. Action research focuses upon identified problems in a local school. A team approach devises a research plan to remedy the problem. Information gathered may come from educational journals and university level textbooks, audio visual aids, as well as CDs and DVDs. Data is gathered, analyzed, and summarized. Action research stresses using feasible methods of proceeding in dong research, Generally, this will not involve technical experimental studies involving a treatment and a control group, but rather use less expensive, quality approaches such as indepth surveying of recent professional literature. The summaries and conclusions may be implemented more readily in the classroom setting.

Action research may be done in a plethora of areas such as grouping students for instruction, new plans of mathematics instruction, student experimentation in science, learning stations, scripted reading, and use of primary sources in social studies, among others.

Duke (2006), studied characteristics common to three or more research studies which were successfully used in aiding low performing schools (number of studies listed in parentheses):

- *Assistance*. Students experiencing problems with learning received prompt assistance (4).
- *Collaboration*. Teachers were expected to work together at various levels to plan, monitor student progress, and provide assistance to struggling readers (4).
- *Data driven decision-making*. Data on student achievement were used on a regular basis to make decisions regarding resource allocations, student needs, teacher effectiveness and other matters (4).

- *Leadership*. The actions of principals and teacher leaders set the tone for the school improvement process (4).
- *Organizational structure*. Aspects of school organization — including roles, teams, and planning processes — were adjusted to support efforts to raise student achievement (4).
- *Staff development*. Teachers received training on a continuing basis in order to support and sustain school improvement efforts (4).
- *Alignment*. Tests were aligned with curriculum content, and curriculum content was aligned with instruction (3).
- *Assessment*. Students were assessed on a regular basis to determine their progress in learning required content (3).
- *High expectations*. Teachers insisted that students were capable of doing high quality academic work (3).
- *Parent involvement*. School personnel reached out to parents to keep then apprised of their child's progress and to enlist them in supporting school improvement efforts (3).
- *Scheduling*. Adjustments were made in the daily schedule in order to increase time for academic work, especially the key areas of reading and mathematics (3).

The model schools concept may be studied in diverse ways. A variety of resources need to be available for indepth study. Chosen examples from the study may be implemented in classroom teaching. Results from the implementation need to be shared with other professionals to improve curricular decisions. Each student in the classroom should then be assisted to achieve as optimally as possible.

REFERENCES

Duke, Daniel L. (2006), "What We Know and Don't Know About Improving Low Performing Schools", *Phi Delta Kappan*, 87 (10), 729-739.

Ediger, Marlow, and D. Bhaskara Rao (2006), *Issues in School Curriculum*. New Delhi, India: Discovery Publishing House.

Fuller, Bruce (August 9, 2006), "Accountability Plus", *Education Week*, 25 (44), 32-34.

Poutiatine, M. (2005), *Finding Common Threads: Summary of the Research on Teacher Formation and the Courage to Teach*. Rainbo Island, Washington: Center for Courage and Renewal.

Shields, P.M., *et. al.* (1999), *The Status of the Teaching Profession*, Santa Cruz, California: The Center for the Future of Teaching and Learning.

21

GOALS IN SCHOOL CURRICULUM

There are different schools of thought in education each of which lead to diverse objectives of instruction. Teachers, supervisors, and administrators need to view these considerations to notice if the local curriculum needs modification, inclusion, or change. The considerations to be discussed view the curriculum from different perspectives.

GOALS IN SCHOOL CURRICULUM

No Child Left Behind (NCLB) is a federal law as of 2002. Here, each state has developed mandated objectives for students to achieve. The mandated law emphasizes the testing of students in mathematics and reading in grades three through eight and an exit test in high school. Students need to pass each grade level test to be promoted as well as the exit test to receive a high school diploma. Beliefs inherent in NCLB include that what is known can be measured. Percentiles and grade equivalents may reveal learner achievement in measurable terms. Additional beliefs include the following:

- important learnings can be identified for all students to achieve
- student subject matter knowledge and skill acquisition need to be measured to notice progress
- learner achievement in two curriculum areas alone, reading and mathematics, provide the foundation for ascertaining progress. Science is to be added in the 2007-2008 school year.
- precise cut off points can be determined to indicate progress or lack thereof
- student achievement may be upped with mandated testing and AYP requirements.

Adequate yearly progress (AYP) criteria must be met by each class/school. AYP standards are determined by the state department of education and indicate the categories of students which must achieve definite standards, in numerical terms. These separate categories to meet AYP include English Language Learners, and special needs children. The expectations are as high for these two categories of children as compared to the others in the school setting including the talented and the gifted. After being declared "deficient" for two years in failing to meet AYP criteria, the school needs to notify the parents that students may receive free tutoring or transfer to a satisfactory school which has met all AYP requirements.

No Child Left Behind is based on the thinking of behaviourism. B.F. Skinner was a leading exponent of this school of thought. Morris and Pai wrote (1976).

According Skinner then the most important task of the teacher is to arrange conditions under which desired learning can occur. Considering the fact that teachers are to bring about changes in extremely complex behaviours, they should be specialists in human behaviour. Effective and efficient manipulations of the multitude of variables affecting children's intellectual and social behaviours cannot be accomplished by trial and error alone, nor should such work be based on the teacher's personal experiences, since this covers only a range of circumstances. Consequently, a scientific study of human behaviour is vital in the improvement of teaching because it provides accurate and reliable information about learning and leads to the development of new instructional materials, methods, and techniques since an empirical analysis of the teaching process is essential, for it clarifies the teacher's responsibility through a series of small and progressive approximations. This approach makes teaching practices more specific, thereby facilitating a more effective evaluation.

No Child Left Behind evaluation results come from testing and are stated numerically. Vague statements of student progress are not accepted; precisions is wanted instead.

EDUCATING FOR CITIZENSHIP

Educators who favour a strong emphasis placed upon good citizenship believe that this goal is completely omitted in NCLB. If "what gets tested gets taught", then a vital ingredient in school is missing and that is people relating to each other in positive ways in the societal arena. What is more salient than good human relations? Students need to have knowledge of their respective rights and responsibilities. Standards of conduct need to be developed and posted on the classroom wall for all to follow. When they are not being followed, diagnosis and remediation must occur. The standards need to be enforced. Co-operative development of classroom rules and enforcement thereof is necessary. Citizenship behaviour might well be emphasized through:

- a comprehensive study of the Constitution, The Bill of Rights, as well as units of study in local, state, and federal government taught on each grade level
- the practice in every day living in the classroom of quality behaviour
- integrating citizenship behaviours in each curriculum area
- working in committees whereby respect and acceptance of others is in evidence
- students assisting each other, when needed, in classroom work
- co-operative endeavours and yet the talents of individuals must also be recognized
- omitting rudeness, retaliation, and impolite behaviour.

With good citizenship, students should achieve at a higher level of accomplishment. Instead of worrying about negative behaviour and being mistreated, the learner may concentrate more on the academic. Discussing situations in society where good behaviour was stressed, the student becomes increasingly aware of needed criteria for quality citizenship.

There are a plethora of concerns of those advocating students learning to become good citizens. Environmental education is a major concern. Deb and Bhattacharya (2006), wrote the following:

> The accomplishment of an eco-friendly environment, sustained and equitable development, and protection and preservation of biodiversity remains the greatest challenge to humanity today. The essential task of

development to provide access to resources and opportunities for a better quality life for all people; but recent years have witnessed rising concern about whether development would lead to serious enviormental damages, or whether environmental restraints would limit development. Therefore, appropriate policies, programs, and technologies must be adopted to encourage efficient use of resources that lead to less environmental harm to society. In order to achieve this objectives, a re-orientation of the education system is required which will lead to a heightened sense of responsibility in individuals and groups towards an eco-friendly and sustainable development. This is possible only when environmental issues are identified scientifically understood and appropriate solutions applied for their improvement; into the way people perform their trade, profession or occupation".

EMPHASIZING THE FINE ARTS

There are selected educators who place strong emphasis upon the fine arts in the curriculum. They, of course, do not oppose the teaching of teaching, mathematics, science, and the social studies, but do say that the fine arts are receiving no or very minimal emphasis in the school curriculum. The fine arts, consisting of creative endeavours such as drama, dance, music (the performing arts), and the visual arts are being left out due to the strong emphasis being placed upon testing in reading and mathematics, due to No Child Left Behind federal mandate. In educational journals there are reports of teachers drilling students in preparation for NCLB tests in grades three through eight, and the exit test. There is much pressure on teachers and administrators to help students achieve passing scores on state mandated tests, not only for students being promoted to the next grade level but also for meeting AYP standards.

The question arises, "Why are the fine arts important?" There are several reasons:

- they meet needs of selected learners and provides for individual differences
- they assist learners to make choices as to what to pursue in terms of vocations, and avocations
- they help to provide for recreational needs of individuals
- they assist in making for a well rounded education
- they emphasize the concept of "beauty" in life
- they stress a style of learning with creativity as a focal point
- they provide for individual differences.

PROBLEM SOLVING IN SCHOOL AND IN SOCIETY

Individuals are continually attempting to solve problems in life. Society expects persons to be able to solve their very own personal and social problems. In each of the above schools of thought, elements of problem solving are involved, but the focal point emphasizes other philosophies. Perhaps, good citizenship behaviour comes closest to stressing problem solving. There are, of course, dilemma situations in being a good citizen and choices that need to be made. In the school curriculum, students identify questions and problems, in context, worthy of securing solutions. In an ongoing unit on China in the social studies, students may choose problems such as the following for solution:

- Why has China recently become a leading nation economically?

- Why did China build a large damn in the vulnerable Three Rivers Gorge on the Yangsee?
- How has China upped their capacity for crop production?

For each of these problem areas, an hypothesis needs to be developed. The hypothesis is tentative. Information, from a variety of reference sources, needs to be gathered, analyzed and synthesized in providing a solution. This results in testing the hypothesis. The hypothesis is accepted, modified, or refuted based on information gathered. Problem solving emphasizes:

- students working co-operatively on identifying and solving problems
- knowledge not being an absolute, but subject to change
- students learning to use different sources of information
- facts, concepts, and generalizations obtained are used in the solving of problems. Subject matter is not learned for its own sake.

Pertaining to problem solving of which John Dewey was a leading exponent, Eichelberger (1989), wrote:

> "The relationship between knowledge and reality (truth) that is used by many researchers today is that of the pragmatist. John Dewey was a principle spokesman for this position, which states that all knowledge is produced by human beings and that we can never distinguish knowledge and truth. In empirical research, this means if something works in practice then it is true, or we can assume that it is true. A truth (knowledge) that is not supported by further empirical study will be modified or discarded".

There are additional philosophies which may be brought into the school curriculum. These include the following:

- William Heard Kilpatrick and the project method. This is a learning by doing approach whereby pupils choose projects involving student purpose in making the selection, planning the steps in doing the project, carrying out the project, and assessing the finished product in terms of desired criteria.
- William Chandler Bagley and essentialism whereby the basics are carefully identified and taught. Trivia is omitted.
- Jerome Bruner and the structure of knowledge. The structure represents key, main ideas identified by subject matter specialists and made available to teachers for teaching students.
- Jean Piaget and developmental psychology. Children go through different stages in the maturation process. The curriculum then needs adaptation to the psychomotor stage (birth through eighteen months); pre-operational level (eighteen months to seven years of age); stage of concrete operations (seven years to eleven years of age); and abstract thought (eleven years and up) (Ediger and Rao, 2003).

REFERENCES

Deb, S.K., and N. Bhattacharya (2006), "Perspective on Environmental Education: Challenge to Civilization", *Edutracks*, 6 (3), 9 -11. Published in India.

Ediger, Marlow, and D.B. Rao (2003), *Philosophy and Curriculum*. New Delhi, India: Discovery Publishing House, pp. 69-85.

Eichelberger, Tony R. (1989), *Disciplined Inquiry: Understanding and Doing Educational Research*. New York: Longman, Inc., p. 11.

Morris, Van Cleve, and Young Pai (1976), *Philosophy and the American School*. Boston Houghton Mifflin Company, 340.

22

ISSUES IN SCHOOL CURRICULUM

There are a plethora of issues in education which have pros and cons. These will be analyzed. Hopefully, a synthesis may be reached. The issues are salient and certainly can and do chart directions in education. It is important that educators are knowledgeable about these issues and develop an informed opinion on each.

ISSUES FOR CONSIDERATION

First, where should schools place major emphasis on—closing the achievement gap between the more privileged versus children from poorer economic circumstances or providing better education for upper income children. Strong arguments can be made for each. Closing the gap in school achievement is frequently mentioned in educational literature as being highly relevant. Children at the lower end of the continuum need to experience a quality education so that they may rise on the socio economic level and be trained for well paying jobs at the workplace. Living in poverty or at menial position robs the person of the many economic benefits in society. The basic necessities of life such as food, clothing, medical care, and shelter are in poor quality or ineffective for the poorest in society. Reading materials in the home might be lacking completely. Travel to educational places, too, are not in the offing. The essential notion that one does not have what many privileged people have is certainly defeating. Working at one, two, and even three low paying jobs is certainly not enticing or motivating (See Maslow, 1954).

Experiencing failure in school is not an attractive alternative. Failing a grade while classmates move on to the next level is defeating. Thus, it appears that it is good to truly close the gap between the privileged and the poor in educational achievement.

Toward the other end of the continuum are those who advocate educating students for optimal achievement so that at the workplace they can challenge workers from other nations in output of goods and services. These educators, generally encouraged by the business world, believe that one's own country needs to survive or remain superior by producing more scientists, mathematicians, and engineers. The challenge presently comes from China and India. In the 1980's, Japan, in particular, and Germany were considered to be leading rivals in the economic arena. Many educators remember when the Soviet Union was deemed to have the outstanding educational system in the world. In 1957, Sputnik, the first human made satellite, was sent into orbit by the Soviet Union. The United States then passed legislation to create the Nation Defense Education Act (NDEA) which provided generous support for schools to be equipped with modern science and mathematics equipment, as well as for foreign language instruction. Teachers taking university level courses in science, mathematics, and foreign language instruction received grants, stipends, and scholarships for attending. The NDEA was truly an attempt to upgrade education and schooling.

The 1981 U.S. national report titled 'A Nation At Risk' was an attempt to challenge teachers and administrators by showing in its contents the mediocrity in U.S. education. No money was mentioned or given to upgrade teaching and learning. This report had a definite negative influence on education. Nothing important came from this report to improve public schools. The contents, again, indicated the importance of being competitive economically with other nations in the world.

The emphasis here is on being competitive. Students need to achieve test-wise at a higher level to stay on top world-wide as far as the United States is concerned. If students do not do well on tests, this shows the downward trend of the United States. This, no doubt, refers to the top echelon of students who are to excel in mathematics and science as well as to educate more engineers. So, instead of better education for the lower level minority students to close the gap, more emphasis needs to be placed upon the best students. The better students will become the future leaders to keep pace or excel that of competing nations. It is a cry of urgency promoted, in part, by the business world. Presently, India and China are doing extremely well in the economic arena (Ediger, 2001).

Questions which need to be answered pertaining to major emphasis placed upon closing gaps in education versus educating for economic leadership are the following:

- might/should both goals be stressed in the curriculum?

- is it an either/or situation or both and consideration?
- should a democracy stress equality of educational opportunity in that all students should receive the best education possible?
- whose interests should be fostered, the business world or democracy as a philosophy of education? (See Ediger, 2005).

Second, should all students be held to the same/similar standard as advocated No Child Left Behind Law of 2002? Presently, special education students are to meet alike standards as compared to normal children. As a separate category, test scores are disaggregated of several categories. Among others, these include the separate categories of special education, and English Language Learners (ELL). The latter two categories of students then must meet the same/similar standards as compared to normal children. The question certainly arises as to the possibility of doing so. There are alternatives here. The special education as well as ELL students, might be assessed in a value added approach. With value added approaches, students are compared with their own individual test scores in sequential school years and not compared to others. Here, teachers and school administrators may notice if there is progress in achievement. A certain amount of progress is to be expected.

Another problem in disaggregating scores is to hold children from poverty homes to the same/similar standards as compared to those who come from a favoured socio-economic environment. Closing the gap in achievement between minorities and other learners has always been advocated and must continue to be an important objective of instruction. The writer's thinking is that all students should be assessed based on value added procedures. Student "A" would then be compared with his/her own previous performance on a yearly basis. Comparing one student with another, in standardized test results, is not fair due to the many differences that exist among learners.

Questions which arise pertaining to NCLB, among others, include the following:

- which is the best way to assess different categories of students when testing for achievement purposes?
- should adjustments be made to ascertain achievement for special education and ELL students?
- are there other techniques to ascertain achievement than standardized testing? For example, port folios, school wide teacher written tests, and recorded teacher observations may be considered as alternatives (See, Calvelti, 2006).

A NATIONAL CURRICULUM

Historically school districts have been managed by local boards of education. The board of education, consisting of lay citizens, is responsible for finances, hiring of employees, as well as the enforcement of school laws and regulations. The school board in return hires a superintendent of schools who then assumes responsibility for school operations. He recommends to the board of education the hiring of teachers and principals, among other employees necessary for school operation and for being in compliance with mandated laws. There are exceptions to this model. For example, the mayor of a large city may be responsible for operating the school system such as employing a superintendent of schools and other employees. There will be close co-operation then between the mayor and the superintendent.

With state mandated objectives, there are differences in what and how much achievement each state requires on NCLB. It will be easier for a student to pass an NCLB test for promotion in grades three through eight in one state as compared to the others, or vice versa. To remedy this situation, there are a few educators who advocate a national curriculum. A national testing program would then have all students in the United States take the same test. The same standards apply then to all unless exceptions are made for certain categories of students. With a national curriculum, the following questions might well arise:

- which categories of learners should allowances be made for in terms of individual differences?
- would the national test writers be too far removed from the local school district to be accessible to parents, teachers, and school administrators?
- when questions about test items and scores arise in any school district, to whom would these be addressed?
- would there be a chance to talk to somebody about the test and test results, other than to a voice recorder? (See, Duke, 2006).

There are many complex questions to ask about diverse issues in the curriculum. These need thorough consideration and a possible synthesis secured.

The writers have chosen what they consider to be major issues in education. There are others, perhaps equally important. There has been considerable attention and concern expressed about drilling students to pass reading and mathematics tests in NCLB. Drill is not a good method of teaching. The psychology of learning must be used in teaching and learning situations. This aids students in perceiving interest and purpose in achieving. Individual differences among learners, too, are better provided for. A variety of methods should be used in aiding students to achieve as optimally as possible (See Mc Kenna and Picard, 2007).

REFERENCES

Calvelti, Gordon (2006), "The Side Effects of NCLB", *Educational Leadership*, 64 (3), 64-68.

Duke, Daniel L., "What We Know and Don't Know About Improving Low Performing Schools", *Phi Delta Kappan*, 87 (16), 720-734.

Ediger, Marlow, and D. Bhaskara Rao (2006), *Issues in School Curriculum*, New Delhi, India: Discovery Publishing House.

Ediger, Marlow (2001), "Effective School Public Relations", *Education*, 121 (4), 743-750.

Ediger, Marlow (2005), "Present Day Philosophies of Education", *Journal of Instructional Psychology*, 32 (3),179-182.

Maslow, Abraham (1954), *Motivation and Personality*. New York: Harper and Row.

McKenna, Michael C., and Michele Cournoyer Picard (2007), Revisiting the Role of Miscue Analysis in Effective Teaching", *The Reading Teacher*, 60 (4), 378 -380.

23

PERSISTENT ISSUES IN SCHOOL CURRICULUM

The school curriculum undergoes continuous assessment. Change appears to be the order of the day in teaching and learning situations. Change agents recommend redoing the curriculum and making needed modifications. Many of these recommendations pertain to the structure of the curriculum. There are key elements then which are at the heart of making revisions. Three structural elements will be discussed, namely the objectives, the learning activities and the evaluation sections of curriculum development (Ediger, 2003).

OBJECTIVES IN THE CURRICULUM

There are changes in determining who is to determine objectives for student attainment Who is to select the ends of instruction? Toward one end of the continuum, the state has taken a leadership role through legislation. At the state level mandated objectives are written for learner attainment. Each state is also responsible for writing their own tests. Testing is done on selected grade levels to measure if gains made by each student are adequate for promotion to the next grade level. Standardized tests are used which contain multiple choice test items, whereby all students take the same grade level test with the same alloted time limits. No provision is made for individual' differences such as for slow learners and special education students. Standardized testing stresses the importance of all conditions being the same for all students on a specific grade level. Toward the other end of the continuum, before the days of required mandated testing, teachers wrote their own tests based on what an individual or team of teachers had taught A variety of kinds of test items were written to measure learner progress as well as to diagnose student problems in learning. Presently, teachers still write their own tests, but less frequently, since mandated tests are given once a year. Selected teachers may also use other procedures than testing, for learners to indicate achievement, such as through drawings, construction activities, and dramatizations. The issue becomes, "Who should write test items, the state level or local classroom teachers to assess learner achievement" (See, Korthagen, 2004).

An additional issue pertains to which categories of objectives should be emphasized in teaching students. Mandated objectives/tests stress the inclusion of cognitive ends only. Lower level of cognitive objectives are generally stressed in mandated tests such as recall and mere comprehension of information. These have answers which are the easist to assess by using machine scoring. Whereas, classroom teachers might well stress attitudinal ends also. Quality attitudes are salient for all learners. Good attitudes assist students to achieve more optimally in knowledge and skills ends of instruction (Ediger, 2003).

LEARNING ACTIVITIES IN THE CURRICULUM

With mandated objectives, the trend has been to emphasize much drill and practice so that test scores go up. There have been school administrators who have advocated that teachers teach only that which will be on the state mandated test. They feel this is what counts since students need to pass their respective grade level tests to be promoted to the next successive grade. Also, schools need to pass the designated adequate yearly progress (AYP) standard, with penalties involved if this does not happen such as being labelled a failing school for two years of successive failing test scores. Mathematics and reading are the two curriculum areas presently which require mandated testing. Science will be added in 2007. This still leaves out the social studies and the fine arts among others.

Prior to mandated testing in 2002, educators stressed balance in the curriculum, meaning all major curriculum areas needed to receive their fair share of attention. Thus, general education involves more than reading and mathematics. It involves a broadly educated person. Students possess diverse abilities individually. These need to be provided for in the classroom. Thus, a learner may show much ability in one or more academic disciplines such as in the language arts, mathematics, social studies, science, the fine and practical arts, and music. In addition, selected students may show ability in technical education with its hands on approaches in learning. A broadly educated person is desired which includes providing for special talents and abilities (Intrator and Kunzman, 2006).

Then too, academic disciplines might well be integrated when problem solving and project methods of instruction are used in teaching and learning situations. Students may be:

- motivated to achieve more optimally,
- encouraged through interesting learning opportunities,
- permitted to select individual versus group methods of instruction,
- challenged to achieve objectives of instruction,
- introduced to and participate in choosing tasks at different learning stations.

Teachers, presently, may still allot time to provide for individual differences in the curriculum whereby each student's strengths are recognized and provided for. They need to be advocates of educating students to fulfill personal needs as well as those in society. It does become increasingly difficult to provide for individual differences and needs as pressures for student achievement mount due to mandated objectives of instruction, which are imposed upon teachers (Senge, 2000).

ASSESSMENT OF ACHIEVEMENT AND PROGRESS

With mandated objectives of instruction determined on the state level, the assessment procedures have been developed on the state level. The assessment procedures tend to be multiple choice test items and aligned with the objectives. A mass number of tests can be scored with computer use when using objective test items. When conditions are kept the same for all students in standardized testing on each grade level, positive differences in results indicate more optimal progress for the involved student. Students are passed to the next grade level if a satisfactory test score was secured. If a school received satisfactory test results on adequate yearly progress (AYP), then the school is labelled as "satisfactory". It must make for negative feelings if one's school is labelled as "failing".

The "one size fits all" approach in testing has been criticized by educators in that a single standardized test determines achievement and progress. Additional approaches to testing to ascertain learner achievement might well include

- port folios which contain a random sampling of learner products covering instruction in different subject matter areas, during a specific interval of time.
- video tapes showing student progress such as in a discussion or problem solving situation.
- self evaluation by the learner of a completed project or other activity.
- objects constructed related to an ongoing unit of study, using rubric means of appraisal.
- art projects completed pertaining to lesson/unit clarification.
- projects developed in an activity centered curriculum (Ediger, 2006).

There are persistent issues in the curriculum within the framework of choosing objectives, learning activities, and assessment procedures. These issues include mandated procedures versus teacher involvement in determining the curriculum. Also included are measurement philosophies versus a more activity centered curriculum in teaching and learning situations. In the area of assessing student progress, a single test as compared to using multiple procedures to ascertain learner achievement is truly a major hurdle to overcome.

REFERENCES

Ediger, Marlow (2003), "Challenge in the Mathematics Curriculum", *Experiments in Education*, 31 (10),185-191.

Ediger, Marlow (2003), "Mentor Teachers", *Eductracks* , 2 (9), 9-15.

Ediger, Marlow (2006), "Testing Versus Portfolios to Assess Achievement", *Oklahoma ASCD Journal*, 13 (1), 31-32.

Intrator, Sam M., and Robert Kunzman (2006), "Starting with the Soul", *Educational Leadership*, 63 (6) 38-42.

Korthagen, F. (2000), "In Search of the Essence of a Good Teacher", *Teaching and Teacher Education*, 20 (1), 77-97.

Senge, P.M. (2000), *Schools that Learn*. New York: Doubleday Publishing Company.

24

IMPROVING SCHOOL CURRICULUM

There are numerous plans presented for improving the school curriculum. What is needed is to determine which essentials need to be identified and promoted. In a changing society, this is difficult to do and will be ongoing. Changes made should not make for anarchy, but rather make for interventions where necessary. What are selected, necessary innovations which should be made in teaching and learning?

NEEDED CHANGES IN THE CURRICULUM

Changes made in the curriculum need to be based upon co-operative problem identification and solutions sought. The focus needs to be on what will assist learners to achieve more optimally. Students must be challenged and encouraged to achieve objectives of instruction, but the ends should be developmentally appropriate and achievable. Thus, high expectations for learners to attain must be reasonable and relevant.

Objectives, too complex to attain, might be scaffolded. Thus, the teacher must plan sequentially learning activities to take care of the gap between where a student is presently in achievement and where the desired level of attainment should be. Scaffolding is a valuable concept for teachers to use in the instructional arena. It does not mean forcing higher attainment, but rather, sequencing learning opportunities properly, so that learners achieve the desired end of instruction.

Teachers need to emphasize positive student talk in the classroom. Too frequently, the teacher lectures to students in different curriculum areas. Learners may not make sense of the lecture. Thus, students should have ample opportunities to discuss ideas and ask questions for clarification, leading toward higher levels of cognition in an ongoing lesson or unit of study. For example, learning to think creatively is important and this may be fostered through brain storming. Thus, if students, collectively, present as many uses as they can for an object, such as a tin can, new ideas then accrue in oral communication. Further creative endeavours are to have students become motivated to tell creative stories, fables, myths, legends, tall tales, fairy tales, and diverse forms of poetry. Written works may also be read aloud to classmates with the use of proper voice inflection, stress, pitch, and juncture (Ediger and Rao, 2006).

There are a plethora of uses for creative thinking. Originality of ideas is needed in order to be able to solve unique problems and dilemma situations. Tried and traditional solutions may not work to solve problems. Novel solutions may be necessary and these may be expressed orally or in writing. Student talk and written work are needed in order to improve in the communication of ideas.

Critical thinking presents further opportunities for orally communicating ideas. Presenting diverse points of view on a topic, debates, rich stimulating discussions, dramatizations, and seminars provide opportunities for oral communication. Student talk should definitely go beyond the rote level of thinking. Hardly does the memorization of subject matter level help when applying knowledge to complex life like situations. Rather, it takes analyzing of ideas, assessing possible solutions, and synthesizing abstractions, to arrive at answers to problems (Tiedt, 1983).

A positive learning environment needs to be in the offing. The environment is open to student ideas and

- encourages learner participation and progress,
- provides positive assistance when needed,
- promotes independent, confident achievers,
- engages students in higher levels of cognition,
- develops interest in life long learning,
- provides for individual differences among students,
- encourages meeting of belonging and esteem needs.

The teacher needs to give adequate time to the student to think when he/she is to respond to questions and problems. Assist all students to participate in discussions and other learning opportunities. No student should fail or be neglected in the classroom. Each student needs to be accepted and assisted to achieve as well as possible (Shepherd and Ragan, 1983).

Teachers need to design lessons which contain relevant objectives, learning activities to achieve the desired ends, and evaluation procedures which assess learner achievement in a valid/reliable way. Each unit needs to have cognitive, affective, and psychomotor ends of instruction. Cognitive objectives should stress critical thinking and application of what has been learned. Affective objectives must stress quality attitudes for students to achieve. Psychomotor objectives stress the use of eye hand co-ordination, such as in construction tasks, art work, and physical endeavours. Units of study must be designed to assist students to achieve broad, structural content, and supporting ideas. Indepth learning must be in the offing so that subject matter is understood and meaningful. Reinforcement of what has been learned is important. Improved sequence in learning is needed so that continuous progress of students, individually, is possible. Diagnosis and remediation should be ongoing. The class as a whole, small group endeavours, and individual work should be in the offing. There needs to be rational balance between students choosing tasks from among alternatives and assigned activities. Evaluation should consist of a variety of techniques including multiple choice test items, hands on approaches, teacher narrative reports, and student self-evaluation should be used in the assessment process (Boyd-Batstone, 2004).

Teachers need to use grouping procedures which facilitate student growth, achievement, and development. There are a plethora of ways to group students for instruction including:

- non-graded methods. Here, the teacher teaches on the present achievement level of students and then assists learners to make continuous progress, regardless of the present grade level of these students.
- team teaching in which the strengths of the individual teacher is used in large group instruction. All teachers then help students in committee endeavours and individual study.

- learning centers approach whereby students individually select sequential tasks to work on.
- peer teaching in which peers teach each other in a given lesson (See Abraham, 2006).

The plan of grouping students for instruction chosen should facilitate optimal learner progress.

TECHNOLOGY AND THE STUDENT

Technology is highly prevalent in the school curriculum. It behooves teachers to be very familiar and competent in using modern approaches in teaching and learning situations. Computers are a tool to assist students to attain vital objectives. They should help students to learn as much as or more than in using other procedures. Inservice education is needed, in many cases, in guiding teachers to use technology proficiently. Skillful use is needed to assist learners to attain knowledge, skills, and attitudinal ends of instruction.

The National Educational Technology Standards has identified guidelines for effective teacher use of technology, including the following:

TECHNOLOGY OPERATIONS AND CONCEPTS: SOCIAL STUDIES EDUCATORS

- demonstrate a sound understanding of technology operations and concepts as they relate to social studies education.
- demonstrate introductory knowledge, skills, and understandings of concepts related to technology
- demonstrate continual growth in technology knowledge and skills' to stay abreast of current and emerging technologies

Planning and Designing Learning Environments and Experiences; Social Studies Educators"

- plan and design effective social studies learning opportunities and experiences supported by technology.
- design developmentally appropriate learning opportunities that apply technology enhanced instructional strategies to support the diverse needs of students.
- apply current research on teaching and learning with technology when planning learning environments and experiences.
- identify and locate technology resources and evaluate them for accuracy and suitability.
- plan for the management of technology resources within the context of learning activities.
- plan strategies to manage student learning in a technology enhanced environment (Social Education, 2006).

REFERENCES

Abraham, Jessy (2006), "Quality of Teacher Education Programs: Some Suggestions", *Edutracks*, 5 (12),7-13. Printed in India.

Boyd-Batstone, Paul (2004), "Focused anecdotal records assessment: a tool for standards-based authentic assessment", *The Reading Teacher*, 58 (3), 230-239.

Ediger, Marlow, and D. Bhaskara Rao (2006), *Issues in School Curriculum*. New Delhi, India: Discovery Publishing House.

National Council for the Social Studies (2006), Technology Position Statement and Guidelines, *Social Education*, 70 (5), 329-332.

Shepherd, Gene, and William Ragan (1983), *Modern Elementary Curriculum*. New York: Holt, Rinehart and Winston.

Tiedt, Iris M. (1983), *The Language Arts Handbook*. Englewood Cliffs, New Jersey: Prentice-Hall, Inc.

25

SUPERVISION IN SCHOOL CURRICULUM

The role of the supervisor is crucial in improving the curriculum. He/she needs to be highly knowledgeable of vital curricular positions, beliefs, philosophies, and trends. The supervisor needs to be skillful in communicating ideas to teachers, administrators, and the lay public. Good human relations is needed in working with faculty, staff, and support personnel. A caring personality is necessary in working harmoniously with all in the school setting. The major role of the supervisor then is to assist teachers, among others in the school setting, in optimizing student achievement.

PHILOSOPHY OF INSTRUCTION

There are several philosophies of education which supervisors need to be highly knowledgeable of. These philosophies provide direction for implementing selected beliefs in education.

Project methods stress the importance of students in committees being engaged in a quality hands on approach in learning. The project approach represents a method in teaching and learning. Active involvement of the learner in doing, achieving, and working is in evidence in the project method. It stresses emphasizing the total person in teaching and learning in the curriculum. Thus, the intellectual, the physical, social, and emotional facets of a person's development are involved in implementing the project method of learning. Thus within an ongoing unit of study, students in a committee decide upon a project. Generally, there is a construction activity which is chosen. The committee makes the choice collectively whereby social development is inherent. Interaction occurs among participants. In planning sessions, the intellect is being used to harmonize ideas in reaching a conclusion on the nature of the project. There are *feelings* which participants possess and develop throughout the project. The project generally emphasizes a construction activity which involves the *physical* facet of development. Collectively all four areas of the intellectual, the social, the emotional, and the physical interact. The purpose for the project, the ensuing plans made, the actual doing and carrying out of the plans, and culminating in its total evaluation are carried out in committee form. There is input from all participants with teacher guidance.

Proper procedures are used in carrying out the project method with

- each committee member participating actively, but no one dominating.
- committee members, collectively, are focused upon doing each activity until completion of the project.

- interest and effort put forth are optimal for each member
- criteria for evaluation of the project are completed by committee members
- teachers being guides, stimulators of student achievement, and models for doing each activity
- a student centered curriculum being emphasized. Decision making is important for the student (Ediger and Rao, 2007).

A second philosophy of instruction stresses measurement theory. Objectives are determined prior to instruction and stated in precise terms. Either a student does/does not achieve the objectives as a result of instruction. The learning opportunities then need to be aligned with the precise objectives of instruction. Student achievement is then evaluated against the specific objectives of instruction. The curriculum becomes tightened among the objectives, learning opportunities, and evaluation procedures. There is much less leeway for student input into measurement theory of instruction as compared to the project method. Key concepts to stress in measurement theory of curriculum development are the following:

- measurement of instruction,
- alignment of objectives, learning opportunities, and evaluation procedures,
- precise data from evaluation of student achievement such as percentiles and grade equivalents,
- an adult centered curriculum being emphasized (See Guilfoyle, 2006).

Presently, in educational practices, the emphasis is upon mandated testing, usually based upon precise, measurably stated objectives. The curriculum then mandates testing in reading and mathematics, only. Science will be added in and for the 2007-2008 school year. There has been much criticism on the limited or narrowness of these involved curriculum areas.

Thus, a third philosophy of education to be discussed involves centering upon the academics. The language arts, mathematics, science, and the social studies are generally referred to as the basics. A solid grasp of subject matter in each discipline is necessary for teachers to teach in their academic area of specialization. Well prepared teachers for teaching subject matter are needed for teaching the basics. Students need to achieve vital subject matter in order to be prepared for college or the workplace.

Academicians in their respective academic disciplines need to assist in selecting subject matter for teachers to emphasize in the school curriculum. Learning activities for students to achieve the objectives need to be challenging for optimal learner achievement. An adult centered curriculum is generally an end result. The debate, too, goes on as to which is better a student versus an adult determined curriculum. The latter may receive elaboration in discussing a subject centered curriculum for the school setting. The former secures increased attention in a child centred curriculum, such as the project method (Ediger and Rao, 2007).

A fourth philosophy stresses educating the whole child. This includes the curriculum areas of the language arts, mathematics, science, and the social studies. It also emphasizes art, music, and physical education. The humanities consisting of art and music, in particular, are stressed by selected educators as being highly important. These two curriculum areas stress creativity as being major objective of instruction. Novelty, uniqueness, and originality are emphasized in the humanities. Students need to experience ample opportunities in art and music.

Physical education certainly should receive strong consideration in the curriculum. With thirty per cent of school age students being over weight, it behooves schools to provide a quality program of physical education. A developmentally appropriate program needs to be in the offing. A strong body with a strong mind should receive much attention in teaching and learning situations.

An integrated approach in curriculum development is then generally advocated with art, music, and physical education together with the basic four academic disciplines of the language arts, mathematics, science, and the social studies should provide for a well rounded person (See Dewey, 1916).

LEADERSHIP TO IMPROVE THE CURRICULUM

The supervisor of the curriculum must be well versed in diverse plans to improve teaching and learning situations. One plan being to conduct a workshop based on input from all teachers in a school pertaining to what are perceived weaknesses which need to be remedied. A survey may then be conducted to ascertain which areas of the curriculum need improvement. The following problem areas might well appear on the survey:

- working with behaviourally disordered children in the classroom
- using behaviour modification with a hyperactive child
- orienting students to taking standardized tests

- using peer instruction in small group sessions
- educating the whole child.

Each of the sessions, pertaining to one or more of the above listed problem areas could involve a general session, following by indepth discussion in committee settings. Demonstration teaching in the small group setting should be included to develop a model for teacher use. The modeling procedure needs to be followed with teacher practice of the model in the regular classroom. Feed back from students might well be presented by the teacher to participants in the workshop.

Ample time needs to be given to each session in the workshop and to participant questions which arise. Clarity of ideas and innovations need adequate emphasis (See Pardo, 2004).

A second procedure of inservice education pertains to having a professional library for teachers in a designated area of the local school. The professional library, among others, needs to have monthly publications from organizations such as:

- The National Science Teachers Association (Science and Children).
- The International Reading Association (The Reading Teacher).
- The National Council Teachers of English (The Language Arts).
- The National Council Teachers of Mathematics (The Arithmetic Teacher).

Teacher education textbooks published by leading publication companies also need to be in the offing. These textbooks should highlight salient information in teaching the different academic and curriculum areas.

Administrators should also have housed in the professional library such journals as the National Elementary Principal as well as the Bulletin of the National Secondary School Principals Association. University level textbooks on school administration, too, need to be in the offing.

Both teachers and school administrators must take time to read and discuss content read. Inservice education may be arranged to accommodate these sessions (National Association of Elementary School Principals, 1990).

Third, professional meetings, state and national, may provide excellent teaching and administration information for attendees. They pertain to teaching of the language arts, mathematics, science, social studies, as well as school administration, among others. Each general session and each sectional meeting has something to offer participants. The content presented may offer food for thought on educational philosophies and psychologies which might then be translated into the school curriculum. Sometimes, the presentation may be highly specific such as performing several science experiments emphasizing a specific unit of study.

The writer has attended a plethora of meetings and has been a speaker in more than 100 professional sessions. The benefits he has received as a speaker are numerous indeed. It takes careful research to prepare a talk on a specific topic. Questions raised, after a talk has been given, encourage the writer to develop more indepth subject matter on each topic.

Fourth, two or three teachers viewing a student's portfolio might well provide a rich inservice education program. The portfolio contains a representative sampling of a learner's dated school work entries. With a table of contents, teachers may leaf to a specific section desired. The following may be studied and evaluated:

- progress made from one entry to the next in a given area such as writing poetry. Growth and achievement may then be noticed and assessed.
- accuracy of diagrams and graphs developed pertaining to mathematics
- write-ups of science experiments which include the problem, hypotheses, evaluation of each hypothesis, and revision of each, if needed.
- neatness and completeness of charts made in the social studies, such as vocabulary, narrative, organizational, and classification charts (See Fatt, 1998).

Possible methods of instruction may be discussed to assist learners to achieve goals in each of the above named areas. This can be a rich inservice education program for teachers. New ideas are then observed in teaching with possible diagnosis and remediation being analyzed as well as discussed.

Fifth, teachers may observe innovative methods of instruction in a classroom. These visits need to be planned carefully so that teachers truly see quality ideas in teaching and learning situations. Hopefully, these may be used by the visiting teacher to improve the curriculum. Which plans of instruction might be observed by a teacher?

- unique plans of grouping students to optimize achievement.
- a new reading program such as Success for All.
- innovative computer applications in mathematics.
- project methods and problem solving activities in the social studies.
- inductive learning in ongoing science units of study.

The visiting teacher should bring back to the classroom selected innovations to be applied in the classroom. These need to be discussed with peers in terms of strengths and weaknesses. Other teachers should benefit from the observational visit.

Teachers and administrators need to study continually new approaches in inservice education. Quality criteria must be used in selecting inservice education procedures. Teachers should benefit from these inservice education approaches and use what is utilitarian in the classroom.

REFERENCES

Dewey, John (1916), *Democracy and Education*. New York: The MacMillan Company.

Ediger, Marlow, and D. Bhaskara Rao (2007), *Reading Curriculum and Instruction*. New Delhi, India: Discovery Publishing House, Chapter Six.

Ediger, Marlow, and D. Bhaskara Rao (2007), *Administration of Schools*. New Delhi, India: Discovery Publishing House.

Fatt, James (1998), "Innovative Teaching: Teaching At Its Best", *Education*, 118 (4), 616-626.

Guilfoyle, Christy (2006), "NCLB: Is There Life After Testing?" *Educational Leadership*, 64 (3), 8-13.

National Association of Elementary School Principals (1990), *Principals for the Twenty-First Century Schools*. Alexandria, Virginia: NAESP.

Pardo, Laura S. (2004), "What Every Teacher Needs to Know About Comprehension", *The Reading Teacher*, 58 (3), 272-280.

26

VALUES EDUCATION IN SCHOOL CURRICULUM

To frequently, knowledge objectives predominate or are the sole objectives in the curriculum. These situations deemphasize teaching the whole child. The student consists of more than having knowledge of subject matter. To be sure, vital subject matter knowledge is salient for the student to possess. Subject matter is needed to make good decisions in school and in society. Decision-making stresses an important skill whereby use or application is made of subject matter. The development of knowledge and skills also need to incorporate attitudinal objectives. Thus, proper attitudes assist in acquiring knowledge and skills. In addition, good attitudes help the student to be positive in life's endeavours. One type of objective still missing is values ends. Without a set of good values, the individual lacks in making moral judgements.

Values provide direction in making choices in life. They indicate standards and norms for every day living. Meaning in life is developed through appropriate values accepted by the individual/group. Wholeness of the individual is inherent when values objectives become a part of the human being. Life then consists of more than knowledge, skills, and attitudes in the school curriculum.

VALUES OBJECTIVES IN THE SCHOOL CURRICULUM

Much time and effort needs to be put forth in choosing values objectives. Careful perusal of the literature on values education must be in the offing. Discussions with university professors, teachers, and school administrators, also, provide input into the development of values objectives. These objectives must be on the developmental level of students. Student sequential success should be emphasized in achieving positive values it is difficult to state values in measurable terms, but gradually learners may become more values orientated as time goes on with quality instruction and models, as perceived by learners. Quality learning opportunities should then be in the offing for students to achieve values objectives.

Which objectives might students then achieve? Among others, the following appear highly viable:

- acceptance of others, as human beings, regardless of religious beliefs, political orientation, and race. Values take time in their development as well as their habitual patterns of behaviour.
- democracy as a way of life needs to be practiced in the classroom, in the school setting, and in the societal domain. Respect for the thinking of others is needed in emphasizing a democratic atmosphere.
- assisting others as necessary in order that they, too, may achieve as optimally as possible.

- co-operation for the good of students in school and society. There are times for wholesome competition. A rational balance between co-operation and competition needs to be in the offing.
- harmonious committee work as well as individual endeavours must be stressed in teaching and learning situations.
- problem solving, critical and creative thinking should be central threads running through the curriculum
- student self efficacy is a major goal of values education.
- honesty in life's endeavours is to be instilled within learners.
- moral education is needed for students to make appropriate choices and decisions in life (Ediger and Rao, 2001).

Values may be taught directly. Idealism as a philosophical school of thought stresses the importance of what is a priori. *A priori* indicates that certain values have always existed as being correct and good, such as truthfulness, kindness, the Golden Rule, and being responsible. These values may then be taught directly since, in space and time, they have remained important. There is no debate on the saliency of these standards. There may be needed discussions on the contextual meaning and implementation of each value in specific situations.

Somewhat opposite would be the experimentalist philosophy which emphasizes that values are developed within experience and within human interactions. It is human beings who make and develop values. Values then are subject to change in time and space. They are tested in society as interaction among human beings occur. Absolute values then cannot be known, but change in values comes about due to uncertainties in time and space. Problem solving is involved to determine which course of action to take and involves identifying the problem, developing an hypothesis, and evaluating the hypotheses in a social and societal setting.

Realism, as a philosophy of education, stresses that if values exist, they exist in some amount, and if they exist in some amount, they can be measured. Here, values to be taught need to be carefully determined prior to instruction and stated precisely in measurable terms. After instruction, it can be measured if students have attained the precise ends. There are standardized tests available for measuring values possessed by individuals. The results are not as valid and reliable as compared to tests measuring academic achievement. Realism emphasizes the saliency of the scientific world where objectivity and preciseness are in evidence. The methods of science are prized highly as the approach to use in securing and assessing data.

Existentialism, as a philosophy of education, stresses the importance of knowledge being subjective. The feeling dimension stresses the importance of internal choices, goals, and aims. It is somewhat opposite of realism. Existentialists look at the importance of every day situations in which individuals face situations of loneliness, futility, the absurd, and the ridiculous, as well as joy and happiness. Choices made in life might well involve feelings of awe, inspiration, fear, dread, and uncertainty, among others. Truth resides within the individual. Respect for others is necessary. Art, music, literature, and the social studies should receive primary emphasis in the curriculum. For example, in literature, students may read about and discuss situations involving poverty, wealth, riches, failure in life, dread in actions taken, and remorse, among others. Subjectivity is inherent in each of these situations. The feeling dimension is paramount in each developmentally appropriate story or novel read. Values are subjective and need to be considered in contextual situations to ascertain what course of action to take (Ediger and Rao, 2002).

In each of the above named philosophies mentioned, values may well be obtained, but the procedures differ. Idealism tends to stress absolute values which have always been true a priori. Experimentalism emphasizes that values change depending upon what society prizes in time and space through sequential problem solving procedures. Realism stresses the importance of identifying precise ends for learner achievement. Learning opportunities to achieve these objectives are chosen. Ultimately, it can be evaluated if the specific objectives have been attained by students. Existentialism advocates that values are derived internally and the individual chooses from among alternatives that which is truth to the chooser. Choices must not be harmful to others.

LEARNING OPPORTUNITIES TO ACHIEVE OBJECTIVES

Learning opportunities should be engaging. Thus, to stress idealism as philosophy of education, historical units in the social studies, should emphasize a study of situations whereby universal values were/were not adhered to. In experimentalism, leaders in history may have pondered problem solving approaches in ascertaining a course of action as in defining the problem, determining an hypothesis, and then checking the hypothesis in action within a contextual situation. Existentialism may be emphasized with strong feelings which were expressed in deciding upon a course of action. With realism, the teacher of social studies may assist students to locate within a lesson five expressed feelings by diplomats in viewing an incidence. These should be specific and stated in measurable terms. A minimum level of acceptance in achieving an objective is stated. For the above, each objective needs to be challenging, yet achievable by learners (See Parker, 2001).

Current events cut across diverse curriculum areas and might well be used to clarify and develop a coherent system of values. Learners with teacher assistance may discuss issues pertaining to global warming. A stimulating discussion with teacher guidance may be conducted on economic development versus pollution of the environment. It is important to have an adequate number of jobs and work for individuals and yet, at the same time, fossil fuel emissions from industry and trucks/cars into the atmosphere pollute heavily. Apparently the amount of ice in the polar regions is shrinking from carbon dioxide emissions. Animals in the polar regions might well become fewer in number and eventually cease to exist. With ice melting in the polar regions, increased floods are a definite possibility in various areas of the world. Climate change warnings have come about on more vicious tornados, floods, and hurricanes. There are those who dispute these findings. Students need to develop sequential knowledge on the economic benefits versus global warning controversy. A variety of concrete, semi-concrete, and abstract experiences need to be in the offing to guide learners to achieve relevant objectives in the curriculum. Motivating discussions should follow in helping students to develop needed values.

A second current events item, for example, pertains to water conservation versus growing more corn to develop ethanol fuels. Corn production requires much moisture as in irrigation of fields. Irrigation has depleted many smaller rivers and lakes of water as well as the water table having gone down to extremely lower levels. Selected states have/ are buying out irrigation permits from farmers in order to lower water usage. Land may then still be farmed without irrigation methods. The writer taught school two years on the West Bank of the Jordan, 1952-1954, at the time when the Jordan River had ample water and even overflowed during spring time. Presently, there is only a trickle of water flowing from the Sea of Galilee in the north to the Dead Sea, via the Jordan River. In return, the Dead Sea is receding 300 yards per year along its shores. Water is tapped on the southeastern shore of the Sea of Galilee for irrigation purposes and then it does not go down the Jordan River to the Dead Sea (Ediger, 1999).

Pesticides, herbicides, and other weed control methods, as well as commercial fertilizers, have made for increased productivity of agricultural crops. Too many agricultural products were shared with insects and weeds. The opposite effect has been pollution of streams, waterways, creeks, and other bodies of water. Wildlife has suffered in numbers due to toxic chemicals being used on farm land. In some cases, mutations of wild life has been in evidence from farm chemicals being used. Many birds and wild life have been killed from the use of selected agricultural chemicals. Somehow, there needs to be a balance between keeping harmful weeds and insects in check and maintaining clean water sources. Agricultural chemicals have been used excessively and beyond the recommended amount for spraying farm crops for harmful weeds/insects, and obnoxious shrubs.

There is disagreement over the reintroduction of wild life to a given area. In the state of Wyoming, among others, wolves have been reintroduced as advocated by nature advocates and sponsors. However, ranchers fear the loss of calves and older cattle from predators. It is good to have wild life and protect the natural environment, but it is also salient to have an adequate food supply. Supporters of the natural environment and farmers may be at opposite ends of the continuum in terms of achieving objectives. What kind of balance can be maintained here?

Farm land is eroding excessively in a plethora of places. This may be hilly land or even level land, the latter being good for crop production. Hilly land should be seeded to grass to prevent erosion of soil. It may then be used for grazing of livestock. However, overgrazing of pasture lands must be avoided. If overgrazed, pasture land turns into weed patches of diverse kinds. Trees also need to be planted to prevent! minimize soil erosion. For tillable land, there needs to be terraces in some areas where plowing, disking, and seeding is done on contours rather than up and down slopes. Grassed waterways should be seeded in small, hilly areas where level land, otherwise is tilled. These grassed waterways collect the runoff moisture from rainfall and lead the water to drainage in a ditch. Soil erosion then is avoided since the grassed waterway with its gentle slope, basically, does not erode in disposing of excess water.

Too frequently, quality level farm land is used in building houses and shopping malls, among other structures. It is more difficult and more expensive to build where the land is hillier. Land taken out of production, presently and used for building purposes, some day may be needed to produce food and fiber. There is ample food available now, but it is not distributed in an equitable manner. Many poor people are an end result (See Evans and Saxe, 1996).

Land fill areas are becoming too numerous in being filled with waste products. Much of these waste products could be recycled. For example, used newspapers could be placed in separate bags for recycling, plastic materials may be separated from other waste products, as well as electronic waste from others. Electronic wastes such as discarded computers and printers, as well as cell phones, among others, should be placed into separate containers for recycling purposes. Cities, of course, must adopt a ruling and provide for these kinds of disposal services. This would greatly reduce waste products at land fill areas. What can be recycled may then be used again. Cities are running short of disposal places for waste products, but there are costs involved for new satisfactory, ways of disposing waste products.

There are a plethora of problems involved in saving our environment. A high standard of living is desired by most people and this requires the heavy use of natural resources. Will these resources always be available or will rationing/ limiting ultimately come to be? Students need to study involved issues and come up with viable solutions based on critical and creative thinking, as well as problem solving.

REFERENCES

Ediger, Marlow, and D. Bhaskara Rao (2001), *Teaching Social Studies Successfully*. New Delhi, India: Discovery Publishing House.

Ediger, Marlow, and D. Bhaskara Rao (2002), *Philosophy and Curriculum*. New Delhi, India: Discovery Publishing House.

Ediger, Marlow (1999), *The Holy Land. Kirksville,* Missouri: Simpson Publishing Company.

Evans, Ronald, and David Saxe, Eds. (1996). *Handbook on Teaching Social Issues*. Washington, DC: National Council for the Social Studies.

Parker, Walter C. (2001), *Social Studies in Elementary Education. Upper Saddle River,* New Jersey: Prentice-Hall, Inc. Chapter Three.

27

MENTAL HEALTH AND SCHOOL CURRICULUM

The whole student needs to be developed in the curriculum. Teaching and learning situations must reflect quality knowledge, skills, and attitudinal objectives of instruction. Each of these categories is important and the latter should not be minimized. Quality attitudes assist students to achieve more optimally in the knowledge and skills domains. They also help learners to get along well with others. Sometimes, students do well in knowledge and skills achievement but fail to work effectively in a group situation. Later at the workplace, individuals have lost jobs due to not getting along. They have shown patterns of rude behaviours along with being haughty, mean, and brutish in relating to others. It behooves the teacher to plan objectives, learning activities, and appraisal procedures which guide quality learner behaviour.

The Association for Supervision and Curriculum Development (ASCD) in their report titled *New Compact* state the following:

"Current educational practice and policy focus overwhelmingly on academic achievement. This achievement, however, is one element of student learning and development, and only a part of any complete system of educational accountability".

That's the starting joint for a provocative and compelling new report from ASCD's Commission on the Whole Child. *The Learning Compact Redefined: A Call to Action*, offers a vision for education reform that embraces all the factors that influence children's lives and development.

The report's recommendations to local, state, and federal policymakers recognize that academic achievement is crucial but cannot happen without significant emphasis on student health, the school environment, student engagement, personalized learning, skilled and caring educators, and outcomes beyond formal schooling. Significantly, it calls upon the communities in which children live to support programs and policies that ensure success for all learners.

The ASCD learners say the report's recommendations can help close the achievement gap for poor and minority students by shining the spotlight on the issues that most affect learning (ASCD, March 2007).

CRITERIA FOR TEACHING AND LEARNING

There are selected guidelines which the writer will emphasize in assisting in the development of quality mental health among students. These standards pertain to stressing a wholesome learning environment in the classroom and school. Students need to experience that which reflects developing the whole child such as the mental, emotional, physical, and social. Thus, learners need to experience a classroom environment with the following involved criteria:

- *Interest in ongoing learning opportunities.* Interest is a powerful factor in achievement of knowledge and skills. It assists the learner in developing readiness for learning as well as in persevering until the activity has been completed. Each learning experience can be made interesting to the learner. With ingenuity and imagination, teachers and students, co-operatively, may design activities which attract, sustain, and culminate in interesting experiences. Learning opportunities which stress developing good attitudes need thought, planning, as well as implementation. The curriculum needs to be open ended to provide learner input and choice in selecting what is of interest. Voluntary participation with an inward desire to learn stresses the opposite of forcing learning and is a mental health indicator.
- *Meaning in activities pursued.* The ongoing lessons and units of study need to make sense to the student. Rote learning and memorization tend not to capture learner attention. They tend to make for restless inattentive children who do not appear to be engaged in what is being presented. Rather, meaning in learning stresses that students understand what is taught. To make sense and understand that which is taught emphasizes a meaningful curriculum. Mental health is promoted when students perceive the relevancy of active participation in a meaningful curriculum.
- *Purpose in achieving knowledge and skills.* Students need to perceive reasons for participating in ongoing tasks. Many times, learners may feel that tasks are assigned for the sake of doing so, rather than for purposeful learning. The student needs to experience readiness

for the ensuing learning opportunity. Within the readiness factor, student background information is activated. The new content/skills to be learned are then related to previous learnings. This relationship needs to be connected to the self and to the community. The purpose in learning is personalized and involves caring teachers. A mentally healthy child has feelings that people care for each other and develop purpose in learning.

- *A safe learning environment*. Students need to feel free physically and emotionally in ongoing activities. They need to feel liked and not abused in any way. Abuse includes bullying. Selected schools, too frequently, have not had policies in effect which prohibit bullying. Insecurity results on the part of a learner when he/she is bullied in the hallways, school grounds, and even in the classroom. The bully hurts the self as well as others. Emotional scars might well result, especially to the one experiencing a bully.

Abuse from the home setting needs to be reported to the proper authorities. The marks on the child's body, such as bruises received from physical abuse, must be reported to social service workers. Maslow (1954) presented an excellent model to provide for the needs of children. These include proper nutrition, appropriate clothing, as well as adequate sleep and rest; safety needs met in school as well as in society; belonging needs such as feeling that one is a part of a group; and esteem needs such as feeling valued for contributions made. The student might well then experience self actualization:

- *Success in learning*. Each student should fell success in achieving knowledge and skills objectives. Feelings of failure make for a lack of achievement and enjoyment.

Sequence in learning assists the learner to experience a curriculum of success (Ediger and Rao, 2004).

The above enumerated items are guidelines for teachers to follow in teaching and learning situations to optimize student achievement. These guidelines when followed emphasize student and teacher mental health in the classroom. The psychology of learning is then in the offing.

LEARNING ACTIVITIES TO ACHIEVE OBJECTIVES

Learning activities to achieve objectives need to follow the psychology of learning tenets. Each student must be respected and accepted to attain as optimally as possible. Gewertz (2007) wrote the following pertaining to a school advisory program:

> When Bronz Lab opened in 2004, it was yet another small school determined to make advisory work. It grabbed a bit of space inside the 2,600 student Evander Child's School, which was so disrupted by violence and high drop out rates that New York city had decided to phase it out, leaving space for six small schools.

From the start, Bronx Lab used a school model that features "distributed counselling", meaning that all faculty and staff members, not just a handful of experts and trained to advise and support students on academic as well as personal issues. The approach was developed by the Institute for Student Achievement, a Lake Success, NY-based non-profit organization that provides technical support and training to 65 schools using the model in four states. All institute schools follow seven common principles, including distributed counselling, continuous professional development, and an extended-day, college preparatory curriculum for all students.

In the institutes model, distributive counselling and advisory groups do not function in isolation. They are integral parts of a relationship driven, collaborative way of running a high school. That means that relationship between students and adults cannot be just soft and fuzzy enhancements to school life, but genuine bonds that enable students to perform a the top of the game:

> "If you have trusting relationships, you can demand more of students academically, because they know that, in addition to the demands we are making, there is support."

In the Bronx Lab School, teachers are hired to the basis of being willing and able to work closely with students. Subject matter knowledge alone, is not adequate in hiring teachers. Teachers must be able to perform guidance and counselling functions in a closely knit school.

With a close relationship between teachers and students, learning opportunities chosen reflect the positive atmosphere of learning. Good human relations are in the offing and assist students to study in a wholesome atmosphere.

Time needs to be given to sustained silent reading (SSR) whereby the learner chooses a library book to read. The book selected is on the reading level of the student and the contents motivate personal development. Library books need to be easily accessible by genera. Attractive bulletin board displays inform students of new library books available. Encouraging much reading and rewarding these efforts stimulate learners in the ongoing experience. Adequate time needs to be given to SSR for learners to develop sequentially by reading self-selected library books. As much as possible, students need to choose activities, from among alternatives. Thus when writing diverse forms of poetry studied, students should choose the topic to write about. Decision making is then in the hands of the learner with the teacher serving as a guide and one who encourages achievement in a positive manner.

Second, the project method needs to receive attention. Student readiness is important for any learning activity. Within an ongoing lesson/unit of study, the student individually or within a committee chooses a project to complete. The project needs a worthwhile purpose or reason for its doing. Once the purpose has been established, the learner plans the project carefully. The teacher is accessible continually during the project method of learning. The student then carries out the plans to achieve the purpose or objective in the project. Upon completion, criteria are developed to assess project quality. Projects are determined by students based on learner interest and value. Committee work may also be emphasized in project methods of instruction.

As a third example, a mural may be planned and developed co-operatively by students. Murals may be developed inalmost all curriculum areas, but are very conducive to the social studies. Thus, a committee of students may develop a mural based on studying the local community. A rather large paper is placed on the floor for committee members to work on. Inside the mural, illustrations may drawn to show a park with its different plants, paths, sidewalks, and refreshment stands. Details may be put in as needed. Different media are used in mural development such as crayons, coloured chalk and pencils, water colouring, among others. Students, here, learn co-operative behaviours, harmonizing their endeavours, as well as neatness and accuracy of the work product. The mural is generally displayed and other classrooms may see the exhibit.

Fourth, problem solving may involve individual or committee endeavours. Problems are identified by learners in context with teacher assistance and may pertain to any curriculum area. Problem solving skills are salient to use in school and in society. Each problem needs to possess clarity so that solutions maybe found. Deliberation is involved. With a clearly stated problem, students may locate information for possible solutions. An hypothesis is developed which is a tentative answer to the problem. Additional data is gathered to assess the hypothesis. Relevant sources need to be used such as printed materials, audio visual aids, and the internet. If the assessment upholds the hypothesis, then it is accepted. Otherwise the tentative hypothesis is modified or refuted.

Peer learning is very beneficial for many students. Here, learners may change off reading parts aloud of the selection assigned from the basal text. Students who need assistance in word recognition are provided assistance within the involved peer group. Questions covering the selection are identified and discussed. Meaning must be attached to ideas read. Main ideas should be summarized, recorded, and filed for review at a later time. Further use may be made of subject matter read by writing a related poem containing rhyme such as a couplet, a triplet, a quatrain, and/or a limerick. The poem may also be based on syllabication such as an haiku or tanka. Free verse is open ended in terms of rhyme and syllabication and might well be preferred by specific learners.

Ideas gleaned from a discussion may be used in developing a classification chart. Here, items are placed into categories in a neatly made chart. Additional charts include a narrative chart (presents ideas and illustrations sequentially; an organizational chart which shows the lines of organization, with illustrations included, of how federal, and state, governments, for example, are arranged in terms of legislative, executive, and judicial branches; as well as a flow chart which shows a change in a process at a given time such as petroleum and its by product gasoline, kerosene and diesel fuel. Charts lend themselves well for displaying for others to see, use of topics for class discussions, and for learners to utilize content while it is developed into chart form (Parker, 2001).

The above are listed and discussed to present *models* for a quality mental health curriculum. A stress free curriculum needs to be emphasized as much as possible. Ravichman (2007) lists the following causes/affects of stress among children in that it:

- increases the rate of forgetting
- causes truancy and deviance
- increases fear and anxiety during learning
- minimizes interest in learning
- creates underachievement
- makes for unhealthy competition.

Quality mental health is salient for all students. Each student needs to focus on achieving worthwhile learnings rather than worrying or be distracted by an ineffective class/ school environment. Thus, the emotional facet of a learner needs adequate attention to achieve worthwhile knowledge, skills, and attitudinal objectives.

REFERENCES

Association for Supervision and Curriculum Development (2007), *Education Update*, 49 (3),1, 8.

Ediger, Marlow, and D. Bhaskara Rao (2004), *Elementary Curriculum Improvement*. New Delhi, India: Discovery Publishing House.

Gewertz, Catherine (2007), "An Advisory Advantage, at Bronx lab School, solid relationships with educators help students perform at the top of their game", *Education Week*, 28 (26), 22-24.

Maslow, A.H. (1954), *Motivation and Personality*. New York: Harper and Row.

Parker, Walter C. (2001), *Social Studies in Elementary Education. Upper Saddle River*, New Jersey: Prentice Hall, Inc.

Ravichandran, T. (2007), "Stress Free Education", *Edutracks*, 6 (7),10-12. Published in India.

28

HOLISM, STUDENT AND SCHOOL CURRICULUM

Holism in the curriculum is a salient topic for all schools to pursue in inservice education. The whole child needs to be educated in order to have a broadly educated person. This is desirable in school as well as in society. There are a plethora of roles which individuals play in life. These are required or expected of the person. The academics receive primary emphasis presently with mandated objectives for student attainment. However, there are a plethora of additional areas of educational breadth which are highly important.

DEVELOPING A CURRICULUM OF HOLISM

The curriculum needs to possess breadth in order to emphaisze holism and to encompass the following academic disciplines:

- reading to stress critical and creative thinking when comprehending content. Phonics should be emphasized when it assists learners to identify unknown words and not for the sake of phonetic analysis instruction

- mathematics to engage in practical every day meaningful computations operations. To provide for individual differences, number theory needs to be stressed.
- science to understand vital facts, concepts, and generalizations needed to attach meaning to living in a world of scientific progress and achievement. Experimentation and inquiry methods are salient to emphasize.
- social studies to provide for achieving citizens in society, including understanding history with its focus on time, geography with emphasis on *place*, economics focus on *goods/services* to be bought / sold, political science stress on *power* concepts, as well as anthropology / sociology focal point on *culture*.
- additional areas of the curriculum to add include the fine and practical arts, as well as health / character education (Ediger and Rao, 2006).

Rational balance among the above named curriculum areas should be in evidence with indepth instruction involved. To make for holism, integration of content should be emphasized, where feasible. Thus problem solving, for example, may be stressed whereby answers to problems come from diverse academic disciplines. Then too within this framework, art projects and construction work might well involve the fine and practical arts respectively, in ongoing units of study. Reading skills may be developed when subject matter is being read to solve problems. Written work, in particular, becomes salient when important ideas from problem solving are recorded. (See, Knipper and Duggan, 2006).

The psychology of learning must be stressed to promote holism in teaching and learning situations. Thus, in an ongoing lesson or unit of study, the teacher needs to implement the following:

- learners need to be actively engaged to achieve and progress.
- learners must intrinsically become interested in ongoing experiences.
- learners need to perceive purpose or reasons for achieving.
- learners need to be motivated to attain objectives of instruction.
- learners need to reflect upon what has been achieved (Ediger, 2005).

Achievement of students increases when the psychology of learning is emphasized in teaching and learning situation. The student and the curriculum become integrated. He/she feels energized and experiences learning to be more enjoyable. The interests of students make for effort in achieving. Active involvement in progressing assists in helping students to achieve rather that stressing passive learners in the curriculum. Motivated students have a high energy level for learning. Reflecting upon what has been accomplished helps the student to rehearse and retain holistically what has been achieved.

Drill is not stressed, as an accepted psychology of learning, since this emphasizes parts rather than the whole student. Drill has become highly important in the federal No Child Left Behind (NCLB) law of 2002. Here, students in grades three through eight experience much drill to pass annual respective tests in order to be promoted. Many reports, too, emphasize teachers drilling students to pass the exit test on the secondary level. Drill tends to destroy interest in learning. A Joint Organizational Statement from the National Council for the Social Studies (2006), has the following concerns about the NCLB standards:

- over-emphasizing standardized testing.
- narrowing curriculum and instruction to focus on test preparation, rather than richer academic learning.
- over-identifying schools in need of improvement.
- using sanctions that do not help improve schools.
- inappropriately excluding low scoring children in order to boost test scores.
- inadequate funding.

To increase wholeness in the curriculum, school should not be separated from society. Thus, students should have ample opportunities to practice good citizenship endeavours. Classroom rules and regulations should be established by students and the teacher collectively. Much deliberation should go into establishing these standards. Modification and change should prevail when necessary. Standards need to be followed by all in a classroom. Students then feel ownership of rules and regulations to abide by. Good citizenship is salient in school and in society. Students achieve more when the learning environment is perceived as being satisfying and fair. Upset feelings occur when students experience rudeness, bullying, and intimidation, as well as a disruptive environment.

Committee work is important when viewing children and the curriculum holistically. Students, here, experience belonging and are a member of a group. For teachers to guide committees effectively, selected standards need to be followed. Respect for each other's thinking is salient. Otherwise participants might refrain from participating. Each should be assisted to participate in an optimal manner. Put downs and disrespect must be avoided in committee deliberations. Ideas should circulate within the committee, not between two members. Ideas need to be expressed clearly so that meaningful learnings accrue. Participants need to stay on the topic and not digress. A chairperson may be appointed or leadership may emerge within the committee. Major ideas kept by the recording secretary should be summarized and referred to at future meetings.

A holistic curriculum might well be summarized with the thinking of the late A.H. Maslow (1954) when he listed needs of individuals which must be fulfilled in order that each person does well. First, individuals need to have physiological needs met such as having adequate food, clothing, and shelter. No one can do well with inadequate nutrition, inappropriate clothes, or housing. Next in the hierarchy come safety needs. With diverse kinds of abuse, many children feel a lack of security. Safety needs is followed by the need to belong to a group. The psychological necessity to be accepted by others is important. Above that is esteem needs. People desire to be recognized for achievement and accomplishment. The highest level of need is to become the kind of person desired, or self actualization.

REFERENCES

Ediger, Marlow, and D. Bhaskara Rao (2006), *Successful School Education*. New Delhi, India: Discovery Publishing House.

Ediger, Marlow (2005), "Science Learning and the Student", *The Hoosier Science Teacher*, 31 (2), 50-53.

Knipper, Kathy, and Timothy J. Duggan (2006), Writing to Learn Across the Curriculum: Tools for Comprehension in Content Area Classes, *The Reading Teacher*, 59 (5), 462-470.

Maslow, A.H. (1954), *Motivation and Personality*. New York: Harper and Row.

National Council for the Social Studies (2006), The Social Studies Professional, *Joint Organizational Statement on No Child Left Behind*, 194 (5), 5.

29

IS THERE ROOM FOR DEMOCRACY IN SCHOOL CURRICULUM?

Quality objectives, learning opportunities, and appraisal are necessary in civics units stressing tenets of democracy. Learners need to practice democracy in the classroom and school environment in order that meaningful learnings accrue.

Numerical scores are provided for all test results of students. Thus, percentiles and grade equivalents are given as student results from testing. Evidence based education stresses exact scores or numerical results from testing. There are no approximations in terms of learner achievement and progress. One test in each of grades three through eight and an exit test in high school needs to be passed for promotion to occur for students. The question arises with NCLB federal law in vogue, is there room also for democracy in the classroom? Research based teaching is emphasized.

Kohn (2006), wrote the following pertaining to research and measurement:

> "Respect for research (and for science, generally) ought to include a recognition of its limits. While there certainly are people who refuse to concede that water is wet until this fact has been established by controlled studies, significant at $p<.01$, the reality is many assumptions and choices we make every day don't require supporting data. Furthermore, even when scientific findings are relevant, there is a difference between consulting them and depending upon them as a sole guide. Conclusions can be informed by research without being wholly determined by it."

Similarly, it should be possible to question how science, with its emphasis upon quantifiable variables, came to be the foundation for the academic study of learning. After all, educational insights could be devised from other fields of study such as anthropology, literature, history, philosophy—and in some cases, from the insights suggested by personal experience. The assumption that all true knowledge is scientific (sometimes known as "scientism") may be just as dangerous as an aversion of, the scientific method. In short, skepticism, which is to be the cornerstone of science also needs to be applied to science (Kohn, 2006).

DEMOCRATIC VALUES

Democratic values emphasize feelings of respect toward others. Each person is to be valued for his/her uniqueness as well as for similarities of traits inherent between and among individuals. Each individual regardless of race, creed, or religion should have ample opportunities to develop optimally. Ample learning opportunities must be provided whereby individuals are able to relate to each other in a positive manner. Democratic living is an ideal and each individual needs to move in the direction of realizing these and related objectives more fully. Individuals differ from each other in degrees of exhibiting democratic behaviour. Individuals/committees must have opportunities to engage in identifying and solving life-like problems. These problems exist in the classroom, school, and in society. Learners personally and in committees must develop a set of values which give meaning to life and these are useful in the problem solving arena. An adequate self-concept is needed so that each student functions well intellectually, socially, emotionally, and physically. A relaxed environment needs to be developed so that students may function as well as possible. Decision-making skills and attitudes need to be in evidence to assist in learning as well as procedures to be used in learning. The teacher is the supervisor of student behaviour in the classroom and assists learners to become involved in teaching and learning situations (See Dewey, 1916).

Democracy stresses the importance of the following situations in the classroom:

- integrate school and society. Thus, the school curriculum should not be separated from life in society.
- students identify and solve problems in contextual settings.
- problems to be solved are realistic. Clarity of problems in ongoing units of study, developing an hypothesis, testing the hypothesis, and making needed revisions, if necessary. Problem solving is the method of instruction.
- a busy learning environment is in evidence since students secure and apply materials to solve problems.

- education is dynamic and change is a key concept in life.
- all affected by a decision should be involved in making that decision.
- experience is a major concept to emphasize in teaching; the consequences of an act are salient to notice.
- the learner and the curriculum are one, not separate entities.
- subject matter learned is used to solve problems (See Brubacher, 1966).

Democracy in the classroom must not be confused with the following approaches. Students doing as they wish with little/no respect for others. The teacher plays a very passive role and provides little direction or guidance to students in teaching and learning situations. Students, in many cases, determine objectives, learning activities, and evaluation procedures. There might be a highly competitive learning environment in evidence with each trying to out do the others. There are winners and losers in these situations. Then too, toward the other end of the continuum, there might be minimal effort put forth in learning.

With NCLB being in vogue, there might be chances for hierarchical teaching and mandated objectives/ measurement in the classroom. The autocratic teacher chooses objectives, learning activities, and evaluation procedures without regard to concerns of student purposes or developmental levels. The beliefs are that the three r's alone should be taught such as reading, writing, and arithmetic. Rote learning and memorization are emphasized and stressed for test preparation. The interests of students are ignored or greatly minimized. There are rigid rules of conduct to be followed, perhaps zero tolerance with students seated in rows and columns during the school day. Exact answers to teacher's questions are expected. Precise measurement of student learning is stressed. Questions which require critical and creative thinking are not favoured. The teacher reprimands students frequently for misdeeds and feels that being very strict is good teaching and keeps students orderly for learning.

The interests of students are not welcome in class discussions but strict rules keep students involved achieving the basics in the curriculum. Students are to sit quietly and listen to the teacher lecture on important learnings. The teacher is exacting in what is expected from students. He/she favours strong use of textbooks and workbooks as the media of study, largely (See Ediger, 2006).

MOVING TOWARD DEMOCRATIC CLASSROOMS

Faculty members need to be assisted to perceive purpose in democracy as a way of life in school. Inservice education needs to be in evidence to identify, clarify, and implement tents of democracy. Criteria need to be developed by teachers and students, co-operatively, for democratic living in the classroom. Revision of these criteria need to be made as necessary. Learning activities must be developed to achieve the chosen ends. Frequent assessment needs to follow to ascertain if students are achieving the objectives.

Teachers need to report back to the group as to how well implemented plans of instruction are working in a perceived democratic classroom. Thee activities may include the following:

- small group work to select and solve identified problems in an ongoing unit of study.

- a variety of reference sources used for problem solving experiences.
- each committee member doing his/her fair share of work.
- reporting progress to other committees at intervals. Diverse committees need to be aware of progress being made and to be informed of subject matter acquired from other groups.
- reasons or purpose for achieving should be inherent in each committee.
- assisting and accepting each other in committees is salient.
- respecting each other's thinking is vital (See Shepherd and Ragan, 1982).

Democracy is a form of government as well as a way of life. It represents an ideal in terms of how people relate to each other. All have a voice in choosing and making choices. Decision-making then may involve assisting in making rules for organizational members to live by. It involves co-operative development of objectives. Learning opportunities to achieve the objectives should also be decided by class members with teacher guidance. Choices are made from a variety of possible experiences. Each member contributes to the larger good be it within a committee or class as a whole. Students with teacher assistance are involved in ascertaining how a committee or group is to be assessed. Results from the assessment provide information for further decision-making in the functions of the class and larger group.

CONTRASTING PHILOSOPHIES IN SCHOOLS

There are numerous philosophies to emphasize in teaching and learning situations. Parents need assistance in ascertaining the type of education desired for their offspring. New types of schools have recently come into being. Charter schools have as their beginnings in advocating innovation. To be accepted as a charter school, quality instructional plans need to be developed and approved. An approval board should then pass judgment on the plan if it is suitable for implementation. These schools have grown rapidly in number. Innovations based on logical thought have much merit. There are standards then which these schools go by. It has been difficult to know how well charter schools have fared with innovative practices. They do not need to meet the standards which public schools are to observe. A lack of accountability has then been in the offing. Some of the charters have been closed due to misuse of moneys. They could have much merit if:

- new procedures of education, beneficial to students, were, discovered. These findings would then be open to the public.
- innovative procedures of evaluation may be used to determine the effectiveness of the findings.
- the findings need to be written up carefully and be suitable for application in other schools.
- accountability for moneys used by charters must be stressed.

Cyber schools certainly have come in strong for all levels of schooling and in many academic disciplines. An increased number of schools have purchased computers for each middle school or high school student in ongoing units of study. Generally, however, cyber schools are arranged for use in home study for a student. The individual might then work on computer programs at home on the internet. This has many advantages for selected students. The at risk student may work by the self-better at home with computer use as compared to a classroom setting. There would be less distractions. However, the parent would need to supervise to see that maximal effort is being made. Lessons need to be completed at a satisfactory rate. Students have much freedom in choosing suitable times to work on cyber space programs.

Cyber work may be excellent for a high school student who is not offered a needed course in school and can take the course via internet. Gifted learners may wish to complete course work at a faster rate than is possible in the regular classroom. Cyber course work might be an answer here. A well disciplined student may completer course much more rapidly on internet as compared to the regular classroom. A shy student might not fit in with a rambunctious set of students in a public school, but can do well in cyber learning. There are times when cyber students in an area may meet together to discuss progress. Being able to choose a school, from among alternatives, does represent tenets of democratic thinking. However, the opportunities to interact with others is limited indeed in cyber schools. Cyber schools and charters may be combined.

Finally, education for profit, such as the Edison Company, offer course work in selected schools. These schools have a contract to fulfill which includes the training of staff and developing a curriculum for teaching and learning. How democratic these kinds of schools are in teaching and learning situations varies. It is salient to remember that their bottom line is the profit motive. Pertaining to privatization, Burch, et. al. (2006), wrote the following:

> "As teachers, local administrators, and state level administrators work to implement NCLB, it is becoming

increasingly clear that federal policy has become an important driver of privatization. And the focus of the law on raising student achievement by means of testing, data analysis, and supplemental services has brought an influx of new services and products from the private sector. It remains unclear whether the services and products provided by the private sector will have a positive influence on student achievement or on the management of schools and districts, but the opening of the educational market place to an ever expanding array of private vendors will continue to have a dramatic impact on school systems."

REFERENCES

Brubacher, John S. (1966). *A History of the Problems of Education.* New York: Mc Graw-Hill book company.

Burch, Patricia, et. at (2006), *The New Landscape of Educational Privatization in the Era of NClS*, Phi Delta Kappan, 88 (2),129-135.

Dewey, John (1916), *Democracy and Education*. New York: Macmillan company.

Ediger, Marlow (2006), *Present Day Philosophies of Education*, Journal of Instructional Psychology, 33 (3),179-182.

Kohn, Alfie (2006), *Abusing Research; The Study of Homework and Other Examples*, Phi Delta Kappan, 88 (1), 9-21.

Shepherd, Gene, and William Ragan (1982), *Modem Elementary Curriculum.* New York: Holt, rinehart and winston.

BIBLIOGRAPHY

Bhaskara Rao, Digumarti (1994). *Scientific Aptitude.* New Delhi: Ashish Publishing House. ISBN 81-7024-658-X.

Bhaskara Rao, Digumarti (1995). *Animal Kingdom.* New Delhi: Discovery Publishing House. ISBN 81-7141-274-2.

Bhaskara Rao, Digumarti (1995). *Batracology.* New Delhi: Discovery Publishing House. ISBN 81-7141-279-3.

Bhaskara Rao, Digumarti (1997). *Scientific Attitude.* New Delhi: Discovery Publishing House. ISBN 81-7141-381-1.

Bhaskara Rao, Digumarti (1996). *Scientific Attitude vis-à-vis Scientific Aptitude.* New Delhi: Discovery Publishing House. ISBN 81-7141-308-0.

Bhaskara Rao, Digumarti (2004). *Scientific Attitude, Scientific Aptitude and Achievement.* New Delhi: Discovery Publishing House. ISBN 81-7141-781-7.

Bhaskara Rao, Digumarti (2004). *Educational Administration.* New Delhi: Discovery Publishing House. ISBN 81-7141-842-2.

Bhaskara Rao, Digumarti (2004). *Issues in School Education.* New Delhi: Discovery Publishing House. ISBN 81-8356-025-3.

Bhaskara Rao, Digumarti, editor (1996). *Encyclopaedia of Education For All,* 5 volumes. New Delhi: APH Publishing Corporation. ISBN 81-7024-759-4 (set).

Vol. I *Education For All: The World Conference.* ISBN 81-7024-760-8.

Vol. II *Education For All: The EPA-9 Summit.* ISBN 81-7024-761-6

Vol. III *Education For All: Quality Education For All.* ISBN 81-7024-762-6.

Vol. IV *Education For All: Planning and Monitoring.* ISBN 81-7024-763-4.

Vol. V *Education For All: The Indian Scenario.* ISBN 81-7024-764-0.

Bhaskara Rao, Digumarti, editor (1996). *National Policy on Education,* 2 Volumes. New Delhi: Anmol Publications Pvt. Ltd. ISBN 81-7488-323-1.

Bhaskara Rao, Digumarti, editor (1996). *Global Perceptions on Peace Education,* 3 Volumes. New Delhi: Discovery Publishing House. ISBN 81-7141-319-6.

Bhaskara Rao, Digumarti, editor (1997). *Education for the 21st Century.* New Delhi: Discovery Publishing House. ISBN 81-7141-389-7.

Bhaskara Rao, Digumarti, editor (1997). *Reflections on Scientific Attitude.* New Delhi: Discovery Publishing House. ISBN 81-7141-319-6.

Bhaskara Rao, Digumarti, editor (1997). *Success Story of a Primary Eduation Project.* New Delhi: APH Publishing Corporation. ISBN 81-7024-850-7.

Bhaskara Rao, Digumarti, editor (1997). *World Food Summit.* New Delhi: Discovery Publishing House. ISBN 81-7141-386-2.

Bhaskara Rao, Digumarti, editor (1997). *Care and Child,* 2 Volumes. New Delhi: Discovery Publishing House. ISBN 81-7141-394-3.

Bhaskara Rao, Digumarti, editor (1998). *Earth Summit*, 2 Volumes. New Delhi: Discovery Publishing House. ISBN 81-7141-435-4.

Bhaskara Rao, Digumarti, editor (1998). *Adolescence Education*. New Delhi: Discovery Publishing House. ISBN 81-7141-432-X.

Bhaskara Rao, Digumarti, editor (1998). *Community and School Nutrition Education*. New Delhi: Discovery Publishing House. ISBN 81-7141-435-4.

Bhaskara Rao, Digumarti, editor (1998). *District Primary Education Programme*. New Delhi: Discovery Publishing House. ISBN 81-7141-396-X.

Bhaskara Rao, Digumarti, editor (1998). *National Policy on Education: Towards an Enlightened and Humane Society*. New Delhi: Discovery Publishing House. ISBN 81-7141-426-5.

Bhaskara Rao, Digumarti, editor (1998). *Reforming School Education*. New Delhi: Discovery Publishing House. ISBN 81-7141-403-6.

Bhaskara Rao, Digumarti, editor (1998). *Teacher Education in India:* New Delhi: Discovery Publishing House. ISBN 81-7141-406-0.

Bhaskara Rao, Digumarti, editor (1998). *World Summit for Social Development*. New Delhi: Discovery Publishing House. ISBN 81-7141-420-6.

Bhaskara Rao, Digumarti, editor (1999). *International Encyclopaedia of AIDS*, 11 Volumes. New Delhi: Discovery House. ISBN 81-7141-522-6 (set).

Vol. 1 *Introduction to HIV/AIDS*. ISBN 81-7141-523-7.

Vol. 2 *HIV/AIDS-Issues and Challenges*, 2 parts. ISBN 81-7141-524-5.

Vol. 3 *HIV/AIDS-Socio Economic Realities.* ISBN 81-7141-524-3.

Vol. 4 *HIV/AIDS-Law Ethics and Human Rights,* 2 Parts. ISBN 81-7141-526-1.

Vol. 5 *AIDS and NGOs.* ISBN 81-7141-527-X.

Vol. 6 *AIDS and Home Care.* ISBN 81-7141-528-8.

Vol. 7 *STD Case Management.* ISBN 81-7141-529-6.

Vol. 8 *HIV/AIDS Prevention and Care—Teaching Modules for Nurses and Midwives.* ISBN 81-7141-530-X.

Vol. 9 *HIV Prevention Education for Educational Institutions.* ISBN 81-7141-531-8.

Vol. 10 *Instructional Modules for AIDS Education.* ISBN 81-7141-532-6.

Vol. 11 *School Health Education to Prevent AIDS and STD—A Package for Curriculum Planners.* ISBN 81-7141-533-4.

Bhaskara Rao, Digumarti, editor (2000). *International Encyclopaedia of Human Rights,* 7 volumes in 13 Parts. New Delhi: Discovery Publishing House. ISBN 81-7141-567-9 (set).

Vol. 1 *International Instruments of Human Rights,* 2 Parts. ISBN 81-7141-569-4.

Vol. 2 *Regional Instruments of Human Rights.* ISBN 81-7141-604-7.

Vol. 3 *Human Rights and the United Nations,* 2 Parts. ISBN 81-7141-605-5.

Vol. 4 *Fact Files of Human Rights,* 3 Parts. ISBN 81-7141-606-3.

Vol. 5 *Study Stories of Human Rights,* 3 Parts. ISBN 81-7141-607-3.

Vol. 6 *International Meetings on Human Rights,* 2 Parts. ISBN 81-7141-608-X.

Vol. 7 *Professional Training in Human Rights.* ISBN 81-7141-609-8.

Bhaskara Rao, Digumarti, editor (2000). *International Encyclopaedia of Science and Technology Education,* 11 volumes, New Delhi: Discovery Publishing House. ISBN 81-7141-548-2 (set).

Vol. 1 *Science and Technology Education.* ISBN 81-7141-568-7.

Vol. 2 *Science Education in Developing Countries.* ISBN 81-7141-569-9.

Vol. 3 *Organizational Structure of Science.* ISBN 81-7141-570-9.

Vol. 4 *Science Education in Asia and the Pacific.* ISBN 81-7141-571-7.

Vol. 5 *Science and Technology Education for All.* ISBN 81-7141-572-5.

Vol. 6 *Values, Ethics, Talent and Girls in Science and Technology Education.* ISBN 81-7141-573-3.

Vol. 7 *Popularization of Science and Technology Education.* ISBN 81-7141574-1.

Vol. 8 *Science, Power and Society.* ISBN 81-7141-575-X.

Vol. 9 *Information Technology.* ISBN 81-7141-576-8.

Vol. 10 *Teacher Training in Science and Technology Education.* ISBN 81-7142-577-6.

Vol. 11 *Teacher Training in Science and Technology: A Curriculum Framework.* ISBN 81-7141-578-4.

Bhaskara Rao, Digumarti, editor (2000). *Education For All: Achieving the Goal,* 3 Volumes. New Delhi: APH Publishing Corporation. ISBN 81-7648-151-1 (set).

Vol. I *The Global Consensus.* ISBN 81-7648-155-6.

Vol. II *Mid-Decade Review Reports of Regional Seminars.* ISBN 81-7648-154-8.

Vol. III *Issues and Trends.* ISBN 81-7648-155-6.

Bhaskara Rao, Digumarti, editor (2001). *Nuclear Materials: Issues and Concerns,* 2 Volumes, New Delhi: Discovery Publishing House. ISBN 81-7141-611-X.

Bhaskara Rao, Digumarti, editor (2001). *Distance Education in Different Countries.* New Delhi: APH Publishing Corporation. ISBN 81-648-229-3.

Bhaskara Rao, Digumarti, editor (2001). *Decentralised Management of Education: Management of Education in Panchayati Raj and Municipal Bodies.* New Delhi: Discovery Publishing House. ISBN 81-7141-617-9.

Bhaskara Rao, Digumarti, editor (2001). *Electrochemistry for Environmental Protection.* New Delhi: Discovery Publishing House. ISBN 81-7141-619-5.

Bhaskara Rao, Digumarti, editor (2001). *Global Educational Studies.* New Delhi: Discovery Publishing House. ISBN 81-7141-616-0.

Bhaskara Rao, Digumarti, editor (2001). *Global Synthesis of Educational Assessment.* New Delhi: Discovery Publishing House. ISBN 81-7141-613-6.

Bhaskara Rao, Digumarti, editor (2001). *Jomtein Decade of Education.* New Delhi: Discovery Publishing House. ISBN 81-7141-618-7.

Bhaskara Rao, Digumarti, editor (2001). *World Conference on Education for All.* New Delhi: APH Publishing Corporation. ISBN 81-7141-274-9.

Bhaskara Rao, Digumarti, editor (2001). *World Conference on Higher Education.* New Delhi: Discovery Publishing House. ISBN 81-7141-610-1.

Bhaskara Rao, Digumarti, editor (2001). *World Conference on Science.* New Delhi: Discovery Publishing House. ISBN 81-7141-612-8.

Bhaskara Rao, Digumarti, editor (2003). *Inspiring Experiences in Teacher Education.* New Delhi: Discovery Publishing House. ISBN 81-7141-656-X.

Bhaskara Rao, Digumarti, editor (2003). *International Studies in Education*, 3 Volumes. New Delhi: Discovery Publishing House. ISBN 81-7141-647-0.

Bhaskara Rao, Digumarti, editor (2003). *Military Conversion: Impact on Science and Technology.* New Delhi: Discovery Publishing House. ISBN 81-7141-578-4.

Bhaskara Rao, Digumarti, editor (2003). *United Nations Millennium Summit.* New Delhi: Discovery Publishing House. ISBN 81-7141-632-2.

Bhaskara Rao, Digumarti, editor (2003). *World Assembly on Aging.* New Delhi: Discovery Publishing House. ISBN 81-7141-637-3.

Bhaskara Rao, Digumarti, editor (2003). *World Conference on Human Rights.* New Delhi: Discovery Publishing House. ISBN 81-7141-661-6.

Bhaskara Rao, Digumarti, editor (2003). *World Education Forum.* New Delhi: Discovery Publishing House. ISBN 81-7141-639-X.

Bhaskara Rao, Digumarti, editor (2003). *Education, Employment and Human Resource Development.* New Delhi: Discovery Publishing House. ISBN 81-7141-681-0.

Bhaskara Rao, Digumarti, editor (2003). *Successful Schooling.* New Delhi: Discovery Publishing House. ISBN 81-7141-677-2.

Bhaskara Rao, Digumarti, editor (2003). *European Education and Teachers.* New Delhi: Discovery Publishing House. ISBN 81-7141-702-7.

Bhaskara Rao, Digumarti, editor (2003). *Teachers in a Changing World.* New Delhi: Discovery Publishing House. ISBN 81-7141-694-2.

Bhaskara Rao, Digumarti, editor (2004). *International Guidelines on Open and Distance Teacher Education.* New Delhi: Discovery Publishing House. ISBN 81-7141-777-9.

Bhaskara Rao, Digumarti, editor (2004). *Adult Learning in the 21st Century.* New Delhi: Discovery Publishing House. ISBN 81-7141-797-3.

Bhaskara Rao, Digumarti, editor (2004). *Educational Practices: Research and Recommendations.* New Delhi: Discovery Publishing House. ISBN 81-7141-835-X.

Bhaskara Rao, Digumarti, editor (2004). *General Secondary Education in the 21st Century.* New Delhi: Discovery Publishing House.

Bhaskara Rao, Digumarti, editor (2004). *International Encyclopaedia of Learning to Live Together*, 4 Volumes. New Delhi: Discovery Publishing House. ISBN 81-7141-848-1.

Vol. 1 *International Conference on Learning to Live Together.*

Vol. 2 *Globalization and Living Together.*

Vol. 3 *Curriculum for Learning to Live Together.*

Vol. 4 *Science Education for the Contemporary Society.*

Bhaskara Rao, Digumarti, editor (2004). *Reforming Secondary Education.* New Delhi: Discovery Publishing House. ISBN 81-7141-843-0.

Bhaskara Rao, Digumarti, editor (2004). *Human Rights Education.* New Delhi: Discovery Publishing House. ISBN 81-7141-882-1.

Bhaskara Rao, Digumarti, editor (2004). *United Nations Decade for Human Rights Education.* New Delhi: Discovery Publishing House. ISBN 81-7141-887-2.

Bhaskara Rao, Digumarti, editor (2004). *Technical and Vocational Education and Training in the 21st Century*. New Delhi: Discovery Publishing House. ISBN 81-7141-984-4.

Bhaskara Rao, Digumarti, editor (2005). *Encyclopaedia of Education For All*, 5 Volumes. New Delhi: Discovery Publishing House.

Bhaskara Rao, Digumarti and B.S.V. Dutt, editor (2003). *Eduation: Programmes and Policies*. New Delhi: APH Publishing Corporation. ISBN 81-7648-470-9.

Bhaskara Rao, Digumarti, C.A.P. Swamy and B.S.V. Dutt (1997). *Self-Evaluation in Student Teaching*. New Delhi: Discovery Publishing House. ISBN 81-7141-374-9.

Bhaskara Rao, Digumarti and D. Naresh Kumar (2004). *School Teacher Effectiveness*. New Delhi: Discovery Publishing House. ISBN 81-7141-.

Bhaskara Rao, Digumarti and D. Sridhar (2002). *Job Satisfaction of School Teachers*. New Delhi: Discovery Publishing House. ISBN 81-7141-652-7.

Bhaskara Rao, Digumarti, C. Sridevi and K. Vijaya (1995). *Achievement in Social Studies*. New Delhi: Discovery Publishing House. ISBN 81-7141-281-5.

Bhaskara Rao, Digumarti and Digumarti Pushpa Latha (1994). *Achievement in Biology*. New Delhi: Discovery Publishing House. ISBN 81-7141-254-5.

Bhaskara Rao, Digumarti and Digumarti Pushpa Latha (1995). *Achievement in English*. New Delhi: Discovery Publishing House. ISBN 81-7141-283-1.

Bhaskara Rao, Digumarti and Digumarti Pushpa Latha (1994). *Achievement in Sciecne*. New Delhi: Discovery Publishing House. ISBN 81-7141-280-70.

Bhaskara Rao, Digumarti and Digumarti Pushpa Latha (1995). *Achieveent in Mathematics*. New Delhi: Discovery Publishing House. ISBN 81-7141-278-5.

Bhaskara Rao, Digumarti and Digumarti Pushpa Latha (2004). *Education for Women.* New Delhi: Discovery Publishing House. ISBN 81-7141-873-2.

Bhaskara Rao, Digumarti, Digumarti Pushpa Latha and Digumarthi Harshitha, editors (2001). *Biological Warfare.* New Delhi: Discovery Publishing House. *ISBN* 81-7141-597-0.

Bhaskara Rao, Digumarti, Digumarti Pushpa Latha and Digumarthi Harshitha, editors (2001). *Women as Educators*. New Delhi: Discovery Publishing House. ISBN 81-7141-602-0.

Bhaskara Rao, Digumarti and Digumarthi Harshitha (2004). *Adjustment of Adolescents.* New Delhi: APH Publishing House. ISBN 81-7648-836-8.

Bhaskara Rao, Digumarti and Digumarthi Harshitha, editors (2001). *Education in India.* New Delhi: APH Publishing House. ISBN 81-7648-207-2.

Bhaskara Rao, Digumarti and Digumarti Pushpa Latha, editors (1998). *International Encyclopaedia of Women,* 5 Volumes. New Delhi: Discovery Publishing House. ISBN 81-7141-410-9 (set).

Vol. 1 *Status of World's Women.* ISBN 81-7141-494-X.

Vol. 2 *Women, Education and Empowerment.* ISBN 81-7141-498-1.

Vol. 3 *Women Challenges and Advancement.* ISBN 81-7141-497-4.

Vol. 4 *Women and Family Health.* ISBN 81-7141-497-4.

Vol. 5 *Women and International Action.* ISBN 81-7141-498-2.

Bhaskara Rao, Digumarti, Digumarti Pushpa Latha and Digumarthi Harshitha, editors (2001). *Assessing Learning Achievement.* New Delhi: Discovery Publishing House. ISBN 81-7141-601-2.

Bhaskara Rao, Digumarti, Digumarti Pushpa Latha and Digumarthi Harshitha, editors (2001). *Energy Security*. New Delhi: Discovery Publishing House. ISBN 81-7141-598-9.

Bhaskara Rao, Digumarti, Digumarthi Harshitha and K.R.S. Sambasiva Rao, editors (1999). *Advanced Biotechnology*. New Delhi: Discovery Publishing House. ISBN 81-7141-516-4.

Bhaskara Rao, Digumarti and K.R.S. Sambasiva Rao, editors (1996). *Current Trends in Indian Education*. New Delhi: Discovery Publishing House. ISBN 81-7141-311-0.

Bhaskara Rao, Digumarti and D. Naresh Kumar (2004). *School Teacher Effectiveness*. New Delhi: Discovery Publishing House. ISBN 81-7141-782-5.

Bhaskara Rao, Digumarti and E. Sreekanth Babu (2004). *Educational Interests of School Students*. New Delhi: Discovery Publishing House. ISBN 81-7141-837-6.

Bhaskara Rao, Digumarti and K. Vijaya (1995). *A Text Book Evaluation*. Ambala Cantt: The Associated Publishers.

Bhaskara Rao, Digumarti and M.A. Fayaz (2004). *Problems of Primary School Drop-outs*. New Delhi: Discovery Publishing House. ISBN 81-7141-834-1.

Bhaskara Rao, Digumarti and N.V.M. Mohana Rao (2002). *Problems of Mentally Handicapped Children*. New Delhi: Discovery Publishing House. ISBN 81-7141-645-4.

Bhaskara Rao, Digumarti and S. Chandra Mohan (2002). *Sports Management*. New Delhi: APH Publishing House. ISBN 81-7648-467-9.

Bhaskara Rao, Digumarti and S.A. Khader (2004). *Problems of Private School Teachers*. New Delhi: Discovery Publishing Corporation. ISBN 81-7141-838-4.

Bhaskara Rao, Digumarti and S.A. Khader (2004). *School Education in India*. New Delhi: Discovery Publishing

Corporation. ISBN 81-7141-849-X.

Bhaskara Rao, Digumarti and Sk. Johni Basha (2004). *Teachers' Population Education Awareness*. New Delhi: Discovery Publishing House. ISBN 81-7141-832-5.

Bhaskara Rao, Digumarti, V.V. Rao, V.V. Lakshmi and V.V. Krishna, editors (1999). *Status and Advancement of Women*. New Delhi: APH Publishing Corporation. ISBN 81-7648-169-6.

Appala Naidu, P.Ch., author and Digumarti Bhaskara Rao, editor (2007). *Student Feedback Methods*. New Delhi: Discovery Publishing House.

Babu, P.C., author and Digumarti Bhaskara Rao, editor (2004). *Flowers of Wisdom*. New Delhi: Discovery Publishing House. ISBN 81-7141-695-0.

Babu, P.C., author and Digumarti Bhaskara Rao, editor (2007). *Worlds of Wisdom*. New Delhi: Discovery Publishing House.

Babu, author and Digumarti Bhaskara Rao, editor (2007). *Teaching Aptitude of Primary School Teachers*. New Delhi: Discovery Publishing House.

Amala, P.A. and Anupama, P., Authors and Digumarti Bhaskara Rao, editor (2004). *History of Education*. New Delhi: Discovery Publishing House. ISBN 81-7141-860-0.

Bhagya Lakshmi, L., author and Digumarti Bhaskara Rao, editor (2000). *Reading and Comprehension*. New Delhi: Discovery Publishing House. ISBN 81-7141-543-1.

Bhasha, S.A., author and Digumarti Bhaskara Rao, editor (2004). *Methods of Teaching Geography*. New Delhi: Discovery Publishing House. ISBN 81-7141-807-4.

Bhuvaneswara Lakshmi, Gadde, author and Digumarti Bhaskara Rao, editor (2000). *Attitude Towards Science*. New Delhi: Discovery Publishing House. ISBN 81-7141-541-6.

Bhuvaneswara Lakshmi, G., author and Digumarti Bhaskara Rao, editor (2004). *Methods of Teaching life Science.* New Delhi: Discovery Publishing House. ISBN 81-7141-804-X.

Bhuvaneswara Lakshmi, G. and K. Subha Rao, Authors and Digumarti Bhaskara Rao, editor (2004). *Methods of Teaching Biology.* New Delhi: Discovery Publishing House. ISBN 81-7141-914-3.

Chary, K.V.N.B., author and Digumarti Bhaskara Rao, editor (2006). *Techniques of Teaching Physics.* New Delhi: Sonali Publications. ISBN 81-8411-046-4.

Chowdary, S.B.J.R. and Naga Raju, author and Digumarti Bhaskara Rao, editor (2004). *Mastery of Teaching Skills.* New Delhi: Discovery Publishing House.

Dayakara Reddy, V. and Digumarti Bhaskara Rao, editor (2006). *Value-Oriented Education.* New Delhi: Discovery Publishing House.

Devraj, T.A.S., author and Digumarti Bhaskara Rao, editor (1997). *Trace Analysis of Uranium and Thorium.* New Delhi: Discovery Publishing House. ISBN 81-7141-375-7.

Durga Rani, K., author and Digumarti Bhaskara Rao, editor (2000). *Educational Aspirations and Scientific Attitudes.* New Delhi: Discovery Publishing House. ISBN 81-7141-555-5.

Dutt, B.S.V. and Digumarti Bhaskara Rao (2001). *Empowering Primary Teachers.* New Delhi: Discovery Publishing House. ISBN 81-7141-615-2.

Dutt, B.S.V., author and Digumarti Bhaskara Rao, editor (2004). *Comparative Education.* New Delhi: Discovery Publishing House. ISBN 81-7141-912-7.

Ediger, Marlow and Digumarti Bhaskara Rao, editor (2004). *Science Curriculum.* New Delhi: Discovery Publishing House. ISBN 81-7141-321-8.

Ediger, Marlow and Digumarti Bhaskara Rao (2000). *Teaching Mathematics Successfully.* New Delhi: Discovery Publishing House. ISBN 81-7141-552-0.

Ediger, Marlow and Digumarti Bhaskara Rao (2001). *Teaching Science Successfully.* New Delhi: Discovery Publishing House. ISBN 81-7141-600-4.

Ediger, Marlow and Digumarti Bhaskara Rao (2001). *Teaching Social Studies Successfully.* New Delhi: Discovery Publishing House. ISBN 81-7141-596-2.

Ediger, Marlow and Digumarti Bhaskara Rao (2002). *Philosophy and Curriculum.* New Delhi: Discovery Publishing House. ISBN 81-7141-631-4.

Ediger, Marlow and Digumarti Bhaskara Rao (2002). *Improving School Administration.* New Delhi: Discovery Publishing House. ISBN 81-7141-633-0.

Ediger, Marlow and Digumarti Bhaskara Rao (2002). *Elementary Curriculum.* New Delhi: Discovery Publishing House. ISBN 81-7141-658-6.

Ediger, Marlow and Digumarti Bhaskara Rao (2003). *Language Arts Curriculum.* New Delhi: Discovery Publishing House. ISBN 81-7141-657-8.

Ediger, Marlow and Digumarti Bhaskara Rao (2003). *Psychology and Curriculum.* New Delhi: Discovery Publishing House. ISBN 81-7141-691-8.

Ediger, Marlow and Digumarti Bhaskara Rao (2003). *Teaching Language Arts Successfully.* New Delhi: Discovery Publishing House. ISBN 81-7141-.

Ediger, Marlow and Digumarti Bhaskara Rao (2003). *School Curriculum and Administration.* New Delhi: Discovery Publishing House. ISBN 81-7141-709-4.

Ediger, Marlow and Digumarti Bhaskara Rao (2003). *Teaching Mathematics in Elementary Schools.* New Delhi: Discovery Publishing House. ISBN 81-7141-687-X.

Ediger, Marlow and Digumarti Bhaskara Rao (2003). *Teaching Science in Elementary Schools.* New Delhi: Discovery Publishing House. ISBN 81-7141-698-5.

Ediger, Marlow and Digumarti Bhaskara Rao (2003). *School Curriculum and Administration.* New Delhi: Discovery Publishing House. ISBN 81-7141-709-4.

Ediger, Marlow and Digumarti Bhaskara Rao (2003). *Elementary Curriculum Improvement.* New Delhi: Discovery Publishing House. ISBN 81-7141-740-X.

Ediger, Marlow and Digumarti Bhaskara Rao (2004). *Modern Elementary School.* New Delhi: Discovery Publishing House.

Ediger, Marlow and Digumarti Bhaskara Rao (2004). *School Organisation.* New Delhi: Discovery Publishing House. ISBN 81-7141-843-0.

Ediger, Marlow and Digumarti Bhaskara Rao (2004). *Relevancy in Elementary Curriculum.* New Delhi: Discovery Publishing House. ISBN 81-7141-845-9.

Ediger, Marlow and Digumarti Bhaskara Rao (2005). *Quality School Education.* New Delhi: Discovery Publishing House. ISBN 81-8356-022-9.

Ediger, Marlow and Digumarti Bhaskara Rao (2006). *Successful School Education.* New Delhi: Discovery Publishing House. ISBN 81-8356-054-7.

Ediger, Marlow and Digumarti Bhaskara Rao (2006). *Successful School Administration.* New Delhi: Discovery Publishing House. ISBN 81-8356-046-6.

Ediger, Marlow and Digumarti Bhaskara Rao (2006). *Issues in School Curruculum.* New Delhi: Discovery Publishing House. ISBN 81-8356-052-0.

Ediger, Marlow and Digumarti Bhaskara Rao (2006). *Community College—Curriculum and Teaching.* New Delhi: Discovery Publishing House. ISBN 81-8356-053-9.

Ediger, Marlow and Digumarti Bhaskara Rao (2006). *Administration of Schools.* New Delhi: Discovery Publishing House.

Ediger, Marlow and Digumarti Bhaskara Rao (2006). *Reading Curriculum and Instruction.* New Delhi: Discovery Publishing House.

Ediger, Marlow and Digumarti Bhaskara Rao (2006). *Curriculum Organisation.* New Delhi: Discovery Publishing House.

Ediger, Marlow and Digumarti Bhaskara Rao (2006). *Curriculum of School Subjects.* New Delhi: Discovery Publishing House.

Ediger, Marlow, B.S.V. Dutt and Digumarti Bhaskara Rao (2003). *Teaching English Successfully.* New Delhi: Discovery Publishing House. ISBN 81-7141-707-8.

Elizabeth, M.B.S., author and Digumarti Bhaskara Rao, editor (2004). *Methods of Teaching English.* New Delhi: Discovery Publishing House. ISBN 81-7141-809-0.

Elizabeth, M.B.S., author and Digumarti Bhaskara Rao, editor (2004). *Acquisition of English Vocabulary.* New Delhi: Discovery Publishing House. ISBN 81-7141-.

Fatima. Sk. author and Digumarti Bhaskara Rao, editor (2007). *Reasoning Ability of School Students.* New Delhi: Discovery Publishing House.

Gopala Krishna M., author and Digumarti Bhaskara Rao, editor (2007). *Teachniques of Teaching Physical Education.* New Delhi: Discovery Publishing House. ISBN 81-8411-044-8.

Gopala Krishna M., author and Digumarti Bhaskara Rao, editor (2007). *Teachniques of Teaching Education.* New Delhi: Discovery Publishing House. ISBN 81-8411-062-6.

Harshitha, Digumarti author and Digumarti Bhaskara Rao, editor (2004). *Methods of Teaching Information Technology.* New Delhi: Discovery Publishing House. ISBN 81-7141-805-8.

Harshitha, Digumarti author and Digumarti Bhaskara Rao, editor (2007). *Techniques of Teaching Computer Science.* New Delhi: Sonali Publications. ISBN 81-8411-036-7.

Harshitha, Digumarti and Digumarti Bhaskara Rao, editor (2004). *Educational Innovations.* New Delhi: Discovery Publishing House. ISBN 81-7141-.

Indira Devi, author and J. Prasanth Kumara and Digumarti Bhaskara Rao, editor (2004). *Values in Language Text Books.* New Delhi: APH Publishing Corporation. ISBN 81-7648-.

Jalaja Kumari, G., author and Digumarti Bhaskara Rao, editor (2004). *Methods of Teaching Technology.* New Delhi: Discovery Publishing House. ISBN 81-7141-810-4.

Jalaja Kumari, G., author and Digumarti Bhaskara Rao, editor (2007). *Job Satisfaction of Teachers.* New Delhi: Discovery Publishing House.

Janardhan Reddy, B., author and Digumarti Bhaskara Rao, editor (2006). *Techniques of Teaching Sociology.* New Delhi: Sonali Publications. ISBN 81-8411-042-1.

Jayasree, R., author and Digumarti Bhaskara Rao, editor (1999). *Methods Correlatse of Socialisation.* New Delhi: Discovery Publishing House. ISBN 81-7141-517-2.

Jayasree, R., author and Digumarti Bhaskara Rao, editor (2004). *Methods of Teaching Science.* New Delhi: Discovery Publishing House. ISBN 81-7141-801-5.

John Babu G., author and T.J.R. Prasad, G.M. Madhukar and Digumarti Bhaskara Rao, editors (1996). *Problem Solving in Mathematics.* New Delhi: APH Publishing Corporation.

ISBN 81-7648-273-0.

Joseph Raju, B., and G.A. Anitha, Authors and Digumarti Bhaskara Rao, editor (2004). *Population Education.* New Delhi: Discovery Publishing House. ISBN 81-8883-631-3.

Lalitha, T., author and R.S. Prabhakaram, D.S.N. Sastry and Digumarti Bhaskara Rao, editors (2004). *Educational Philosophic Beliefs.* New Delhi: Discovery Publishing House. ISBN 81-7141-765-5.

Krishna G., author and Digumarti Bhaskara Rao, editor (2006). *Techniques of Teaching Physical Education.* New Delhi: Discovery Publishing House. ISBN 81-8411-044-8.

Kumar Raju G., author and Digumarti Bhaskara Rao, editor (2007). *Principles of Primary School.* New Delhi: Sonali Publications. ISBN 81-8411-054-5.

Lakshmi Kumari, V., author and Digumarti Bhaskara Rao, editor (2006). *Techniques of Teaching Home Science.* New Delhi: Discovery Publishing House. ISBN 81-8411-048-0.

Madhu Babu Jampla, author and Digumarti Bhaskara Rao, editor (2004). *Adjustment Problems of Hearing Impaired.* New Delhi: Discovery Publishing House. ISBN 81-7141-831-7.

Madhu Babu Jampla, author and Digumarti Bhaskara Rao, editor (2004). *Methods of Teaching Exceptional Children.* New Delhi: Discovery Publishing House. ISBN 81-7141-802-3.

Madhu Babu Jampla, author and Digumarti Bhaskara Rao, editor (2007). *Adjustment, Achievement Motivation and Academic Achievement of Hearing Impaired Students.* New Delhi: Discovery Publishing House.

Majra, Tabi and Digumarti Bhaskara Rao, editors (1996). *Educational Leadership and Social Changes.* New Delhi: Discovery Publishing House. ISBN 81-7141-320-X.

Nageswara Rao, P. and M. Srihari, author and Digumarti Bhaskara Rao, editor (2004). *Guidance and Counselling.* New Delhi: Discovery Publishing House. ISBN 81-7141-840-6.

Nageswara Rao, P., author and Digumarti Bhaskara Rao, editor (2006). *Teachniques of Teaching Phychology.* New Delhi: Discovery Publishing House. ISBN 81-8411-040-5.

Nageswara Rao, P. and P. Sridhari, author and Digumarti Bhaskara Rao, editor (2004). *Methods and Techniques of Teaching.* New Delhi: Sonali Publications. ISBN 81-8883-633-8.

Nirmala Jyothi, M., author and Digumarti Bhaskara Rao, editor (2003). *Non-detention System in School Education.* New Delhi: Discovery Publishing House. ISBN 81-7141-654-3.

Padma Tulasi, G., author and Digumarti Bhaskara Rao, editor (2004). *Methods of Teaching Elementary Science.* New Delhi: Discovery Publishing House. ISBN 81-7141-871-6.

Pitchi Reddy, M., author and Digumarti Bhaskara Rao, editor (2007). *Techniques of Teaching Social Sciences.* New Delhi: Sonali Publications. ISBN 81-7141-066-X.

Prasad Babu, B., author and P. Madhu and Digumarti Bhaskara Rao, editors (2006). *Psychological Adjustment and Well-being of Tuberculosis Patients.* New Delhi: Discovery Publishing House.

Prasad Babu, B., author and M.V.R. Raju and Digumarti Bhaskara Rao, editors (2006). *Behavioural Problem of School Children.* New Delhi: Discovery Publishing House.

Prasad Babu, B., author and K.N. Rani and Digumarti Bhaskara Rao, editors (2004). *India Pakistan: Partition ????? in Indo-English Novels.* New Delhi: Discovery Publishing House. ISBN 81-7141-871-6.

Prabhakaran, K.S., author and Digumarti Bhaskara Rao, editors (1998). *Concept Attainment Model in Mathematics Teaching*. New Delhi: Discovery Publishing House. ISBN 81-7141-424-9.

Prasanth Kumar, J., author and Digumarti Bhaskara Rao, editor (1998). *Effectiveness of Distance Education System*. New Delhi: Discovery Publishing House. ISBN 81-7141-437-0.

Prasanth Kumar, J., author and Digumarti Bhaskara Rao, editor (2004). *Methdos of Teaching Civics*. New Delhi: Discovery Publishing House. ISBN 81-7141-806-6.

Prasanth Kumar, J., author and G. Sundara Rao and Digumarti Bhaskara Rao, editors (2000). *Open University Student Support Services*. New Delhi: Discovery Publishing House. ISBN 81-7141-550-4.

Raja Kumar, M.A. and D.R.S. Sundari, author and Digumarti Bhaskara Rao, editor (2004). *Special Education*. New Delhi: Discovery Publishing House. ISBN 81-7141-846-5.

Raja Kumar, M.A. and D.R.S. Sundari, Authors and Digumarti Bhaskara Rao, editor (2004). *Methods of Teaching Educational Psychology*. New Delhi: Discovery Publishing House. ISBN 81-7141-.

Ramatulasamma K., author and Digumarti Bhaskara Rao, editor (2002). *Job Satisfaction of Teacher Educators*. New Delhi: Discovery Publishing House. ISBN 81-7141-655-1.

Rama Krishnaiah, D., author and Digumarti Bhaskara Rao, editor (1998). *Job Satisfaction of College Teachers*. New Delhi: Discovery Publishing House. ISBN 81-7141-438-9.

Rama Kumar Ranam M.V., author and Digumarti Bhaskara Rao, editor (1998). *Dukkha: Suffering in Early Buddhism*. New Delhi: Discovery Publishing House. ISBN 81-7141-653-5.

Rama Krishna Prasad and P. Vide Sagar, Authors and Digumarti Bhaskara Rao, editor (2004). *Methods of Teaching Physical Education*. New Delhi: Discovery Publishing House.

Rama Seshaiah, M., author and Digumarti Bhaskara Rao, editor (2004). *Methods of Teaching Home Science*. New Delhi: Discovery Publishing House. ISBN 81-7141-916-X.

Rama Swamy, K., author and Digumarti Bhaskara Rao, editor (2007). *Techniques of Teaching Environmental Science*. New Delhi: Sonali Publications. ISBN 81-8411-035-9.

Ramesh, A.R., author and Digumarti Bhaskara Rao, editor (2006). *Techniques of Teaching Commerce*. New Delhi: Sonali Publications. ISBN 81-8411-043-X.

Ramesh, Ghama and Digumarti Bhaskara Rao, editors (1998). *Environmental Education: Problems and Prospect*. New Delhi: Discovery Publishing House. ISBN 81-7141-423-0.

Ranga Rao, B., author and Digumarti Bhaskara Rao, editor (2007). *Techniques of Teaching Economics*. New Delhi: Sonali Publications. ISBN 81-8411-056-1.

Ranga Rao, R., author and Digumarti Bhaskara Rao, editor (2004). *Methods of Teacher Teaching*. New Delhi: Discovery Publishing House. ISBN 81-7141-812-0.

Rani, S.S., author and Digumarti Bhaskara Rao, editor (2006). *Techniques of Teaching Botany*. New Delhi: Discovery Publishing House. ISBN 81-8411-037-5.

Rathaiah, Lavu and Digumarti Bhaskara Rao, editors (1996). *International Innovations in Education*. New Delhi: Discovery Publishing House. ISBN 81-7141-359-5.

Rathaiah, Lavu and Digumarti Bhaskara Rao (1997). *Achievement Correlates*. New Delhi: Discovery Publishing House. ISBN 81-7141-385-4.

Ravi Krishna, M., author and Digumarti Bhaskara Rao, editors (2004). *Examination System.* New Delhi: Discovery Publishing House. ISBN 81-7141-824-4.

Ravi Kumar, M., author and Digumarti Bhaskara Rao, editors (2004). *Methods of Teaching Computer Science.* New Delhi: Discovery Publishing House. ISBN 81-7141-823-6.

Rudramamba, B., author and Digumarti Bhaskara Rao, editor (2003). *Problems of Teaching.* New Delhi: APH Publishing Corporation. ISBN 81-7648-462-8.

Rudramamba, B. and V. Lakshmi Kumari, Authors and Digumarti Bhaskara Rao, editor (2004). *Methods of Teaching Economics.* New Delhi: Discovery Publishing House. ISBN 81-7141-900-3.

Sambasiva Rao, B., author and Digumarti Bhaskara Rao, editor (2007). *Techniques of Teaching Psychology.* New Delhi: Sonali Publications. ISBN 81-8411-040-5.

Sanjeeva Rao, P.C., author and Digumarti Bhaskara Rao, editor (1996). *A Text Book of Geology.* New Delhi: Discovery Publishing House. ISBN 81-7141-313-7.

Santhanam. T., B. Prasad Babu and S. Sugandhi, Authors and Digumarti Bhaskara Rao, editor (2007). *Children with Learning Disabilities.* New Delhi: Discovery Publishing House.

Sarala M.M.O., author and Digumarti Bhaskara Rao, editor (2006). *Techniques of Teaching English.* New Delhi: Sonali Publications. ISBN 81-8411-047-2.

Satya Narayana, V., author and Digumarti Bhaskara Rao, editor (2001). *Physical Education, Social Attitudes and Leadership Qualities.* New Delhi: Discovery Publishing House. ISBN 81-7141-593-8.

Satya Narayana, B.V.V. and G. Krishna, Authors and Digumarti Bhaskara Rao, editor (2004). *Curriculum*

Development and Management. New Delhi: Discovery Publishing House. ISBN 81-7141-813-9.

Shamsuddhin, Sk. and V. Dayakara Reddy, Authors and Digumarti Bhaskara Rao, editor (2007). *Academic Achievement and Values*. New Delhi: Discovery Publishing House.

Singh Y.C., author and Digumarti Bhaskara Rao, editor (2006). *Techniques of Teaching Science*. New Delhi: Sonali Publications. ISBN 81-8411-041-3.

Sirisha Rani, S., author and Digumarti Bhaskara Rao, editor (2007). *Techniques of Teaching Botany*. New Delhi: Sonali Publications. ISBN 81-8411-037-5.

Sivaratnam Reddy, M., author and Digumarti Bhaskara Rao, editor (2004). *Creativity in College Students*. New Delhi: Discovery Publishing House. ISBN 81-7141-697-7.

Siva Lakshmi, G.V. and G.L. Subbaiah, Authors and Digumarti Bhaskara Rao, editor (2004). *Methods of Teaching Environmental Science*. New Delhi: Discovery Publishing House. ISBN 81-7141-839-2.

Srinivas, G., author and Digumarti Bhaskara Rao, editor (2007). *Anxiety of Prospective Teachers*. New Delhi: Discovery Publishing House.

Srinivas, M. and L. Prasada Rao, Authors and Digumarti Bhaskara Rao, editor (2004). *Methods of Teaching History*. New Delhi: Discovery Publishing House. ISBN 81-7141-.

Srinivas Rao, P., author and Digumarti Bhaskara Rao, editor (2007). *Principles of Secondary School*. New Delhi: Discovery Publishing House. ISBN 81-8411-058-8.

Srinivasulu Reddy, L., and K.R.S. Sambasiva Rao, Authors and Digumarti Bhaskara Rao, editor (1999). *A Text Book of Aquaculture*. New Delhi: Discovery Publishing House. ISBN 81-7141-482-6.

Srinivasa Rao, Landababu, author and Digumarti Bhaskara Rao, editor (2003). *Achievement Motivation and Achievement in Mathematics.* New Delhi: Discovery Publishing House. ISBN 81-7141-674-8.

Srihari, M., author and Digumarti Bhaskara Rao, editor (2003). *Values of Propspective Teachers.* New Delhi: Discovery Publishing House.

Subba Rao, K., author and Digumarti Bhaskara Rao, editor (2007). *School Education Policy.* New Delhi: Discovery Publishing House.

Subba Rao, K., author and Digumarti Bhaskara Rao, editor (2007). *Education Planning.* New Delhi: Sonali Publication. ISBN 81-8411-053-7.

Sudhakar Reddy, M., author and Digumarti Bhaskara Rao, editor (2003). *Creativity in Adolescents.* New Delhi: Discovery Publishing House. ISBN 81-7141-659-4.

Sunil Kumar, K. and K. Rama Krishana, authors and Digumarti Bhaskara Rao, editor (2004). *Methods of Teaching Chemistry.* New Delhi: Discovery Publishing House. ISBN 81-7141-913-5.

Sunita, B. and B. Samadeva Rao, authors and Digumarti Bhaskara Rao, editor (2004). *Methods of Teaching Mathematics.* New Delhi: Discovery Publishing House. ISBN 81-7141-915-1.

Surya Madhwa, K., author and Digumarti Bhaskara Rao, editor (2006). *Techniques of Teaching Geography.* New Delhi: Discovery Publishing House. ISBN 81-8411-034-0.

Surya Madhava, K., author and Digumarti Bhaskara Rao, editor (2007). *Techniques of Teaching Political Science.* New Delhi: Discovery Publishing House. ISBN 81-8411-061-8.

Swamy, K.R., author and Digumarti Bhaskara Rao, editor (2006). *Techniques of Teaching Environmental Science.* New Delhi: Discovery Publishing House. ISBN 81-8411-035-9.

Swarna Jyoti, R., author and Digumarti Bhaskara Rao, editor (2007). *Educational Research.* New Delhi: Discovery Publishing House. ISBN 81-8411-063-4.

Swarna Latha, K., author and Digumarti Bhaskara Rao, editors (2006). *Encyclopaedia of Biotechnology,* 5 volume. New Delhi: Discovery Publishing House. ISBN 81-8356-168-3. (set).

Swarup, Rani, K., author and Digumarti Bhaskara Rao, editor (2004). *Educational Measurement and Evaluation.* New Delhi: Discovery Publishing House. ISBN 81-7141-859-7.

Vanaja, M., author and Digumarti Bhaskara Rao, editor (1999). *Inquiry Training Model.* New Delhi: Discovery Publishing House. ISBN 81-7141-515-6.

Vanaja, M., author and Digumarti Bhaskara Rao, editor (2004). *Methods of Teaching Physics.* New Delhi: Discovery Publishing House. ISBN 81-7141-867-8.

Vanaja, M. and K. Sneha Latha, author and Digumarti Bhaskara Rao, editor (2004). *Student Shyness.* New Delhi: APH Publishing House. ISBN 81-7648-.

Valeri V. Koushouk, author and Digumarti Bhaskara Rao, editor (2002). *A Text Book of Cryogenics.* New Delhi: Discovery Publishing House. ISBN 81-7141-642-X.

Vamsi Krishna, K., author and Digumarti Bhaskara Rao, editor (2004). *School Psychology.* New Delhi: Discovery Publishing House. ISBN 81-7141-880-5.

Veena Kumari, Balusri, author and Digumarti Bhaskara Rao, editor (1996). *Operation Black Board.* New Delhi: APH Publishing House. ISBN 81-7024-711-X.

Veena Kumari, Balusri, author and Digumarti Bhaskara Rao, editor (2004). *Methods of Teaching Social Studies.* New Delhi: Discovery Publishing House. ISBN 81-7141-899-9.

Veena Kumari, Balusri, author and Digumarti Bhaskara Rao, editor (2000). *Psycho-Social Correlates of Achievement*. New Delhi: Discovery Publishing House. ISBN 81-7141-547-4.

Venkata Rao, B., author and Digumarti Bhaskara Rao, editor (2007). *Techniques of Teaching Chemistry*. New Delhi: Sonali Publications. ISBN 81-8411-057-X.

Venkata, Rao, B., author and Digumarti Bhaskara Rao (1989). *A Text Book of Zoology—Junior Intermediate*. New Delhi: Vignan Publishers.

Venkata, Rao, B., author and Digumarti Bhaskara Rao (1989). *A Text Book of Zoology—Senior Intermediate*. New Delhi: Vignan Publishers.

Venkatshwara Rao, V., author and Digumarti Bhaskara Rao, editor (2004). *Problems of Education*. New Delhi: Discovery Publishing House. ISBN 81-7141-841-4.

Venkatshwara Rao, V., V. Vijaya Lakshmi and V. Vamsi Krishna, authors and Digumarti Bhaskara Rao, editor (2004). *Education for All*. New Delhi: Sonali Publications. ISBN 81-8883-630-3.

Venkatshwara Rao, V., V. Vijaya Lakshmi and V. Vamsi Krishna, authors and Digumarti Bhaskara Rao, editor (2004). *Education in India*. New Delhi: Sonali Publications. ISBN 81-8883-858-9.

Venkatshwara Reddy, V. and Narayana, M.L., authors and Digumarti Bhaskara Rao, editor (2004). *Eduation for All*. New Delhi: Discovery Publishing House. ISBN 81-7141-872-4.

Venkatshwara Reddy, L. and Narayana, M.L., authors and Digumarti Bhaskara Rao, editor (2004). *Method of Teaching Rural Sociology*. New Delhi: Discovery Publishing House. ISBN 81-7141-811-2.

Venkashvaralu, K. and S.J. Basha, authors and Digumarti Bhaskara Rao, editor (2004). *Methods of Teaching Commerce.* New Delhi: Discovery Publishing House. ISBN 81-7141-808-2.

Venugapala Rao, K., author and Digumarti Bhaskara Rao, editor (2000). *Teacher Morale in Secondary School.* New Delhi: Discovery Publishing House. ISBN 81-7141-551-2.

Venugapala Rao, K., author and Digumarti Bhaskara Rao, editor (2007). *Techniques of Teaching History.* New Delhi: Sonali Publications. ISBN 81-8411-059-6.

Vidya, C., author and Digumarti Bhaskara Rao, editor (1996). *A Text Book of Nutrtion.* New Delhi: Discovery Publishing House. ISBN 81-7141-309-9.

Vimala, K.D., author and Digumarti Bhaskara Rao, editors (2007). *Stree, Coping and Management.* New Delhi: Discovery Publishing House.

Vijaya Bharathi, K., author and Digumarti Bhaskara Rao, editor (2000). *Educational Philosophies of Swami Vivekananda and John Dewey.* New Delhi: APH Publishing House. ISBN 81-7648-309-9.

Vijaya Bharathi, K., author and Digumarti Bhaskara Rao, editor (2005). *Educational Philosophy of John Dewey.* New Delhi: Discovery Publishing House. ISBN 81-8356-024-5.

Vijaya Bharathi, K., author and Digumarti Bhaskara Rao, editor (2005). *Educational Philosophy of Swami Vivekananda.* New Delhi: Discovery Publishing House. ISBN 81-8356-023-7.

Vijaya Lakshmi, K., author and Digumarti Bhaskara Rao, editor (2004). *Basic Education.* New Delhi: Discovery Publishing House. ISBN 81-7141-881-3.

Vijaya Lakshmi, K., author and Digumarti Bhaskara Rao, editor (2006). *Techniques of Teaching Music.* New Delhi: Discovery Publishing House. ISBN 81-8411-038-3.

Vijaya Kumar, S.J., author and Digumarti Bhaskara Rao, editor (2006). *Techniques of Teaching Mathematics*. New Delhi: Sonali Publications. ISBN 81-8411-039-1.

Visalaka, K., author and Digumarti Bhaskara Rao, editor (2006). *Techniques of Teaching Biology*. New Delhi: Sonali Publications. ISBN 81-8411-045-6.

Visalaka, K., author and Digumarti Bhaskara Rao, editor (2007). *Techniques of Teaching Zoology*. New Delhi: Sonali Publications. ISBN 81-8411-055-3.

Telugu Language

Bhaskara Rao, Digumarti (1986). *Dhrushya Sravana Bodhanapakaranalu* (Audio Visual Teaching Aids). Guntur: Nagarjuna Publishers.

Bhaskara Rao, Digumarti (1993). *Jeevasashtra Bodhana* (Teaching of Biology). Guntur: Nagarjuna Publishers.

Bhaskara Rao, Digumarti (1997). *Vignanasasthra Bodhana* (Teaching of Science). Guntur: Nagarjuna Publishers.

Bhaskara Rao, Digumarti (1997). *Vidya Manovignana Sastram* (Educational Psychology). Guntur: Creative Press.

Bhaskara Rao, Digumarti (1998). *DSC Study Material*. Guntur: Nagarjuna Publishers.

Bhaskara Rao, Digumarti (1998). *Upadhyayudu Vidya* (Teacher and Education). Guntur: Nagarjuna Publishers.

Bhaskara Rao, Digumarti (1998). *Vidya Drukpadalu* (Perspectives of Education). Guntur: Nagarjuna Publishers.

Bhaskara Rao, Digumarti (1999). *EdCET Teaching Aptitude*. Guntur: Nagarjuna Publishers.

Bhaskara Rao, Digumarti (2001). *Bhoutika Sastra Bodhana Padhatulu* (Methods of Teaching Physical Science). Guntur: Sri Nagarjuna Publishers.

Bhaskara Rao, Digumarti (2001). *Jeeva Sastra Bodhana Padhatulu* (Methods of Teaching Biology). Guntur: Sri Nagarjuna Publishers.

Bhaskara Rao, Digumarti (2001). *Vidya Manovignana Sastram* (Educational Psychology). Guntur: Sri Nagarjuna Publishers.

Bhaskara Rao, Digumarti (2003). *Patasala Yajamanyam / Paripalana* (School Management and Administration). Guntur: Sri Nagarjuna Publishers.

Gopala Krishna, G., A. Rama Krishna, K. Subba Rao and Bhaskara Rao, Digumarti (2004). *Jeevasashtra Bodhana Padhatulu* (Methods of Teaching of Biological Science). Guntur: Sri Nagarjuna Publishers.

Krishna Murthy, V., K.S. Sudheer Reddy and Digumarti Bhaskara Rao, (2004). *Vidya Manovignana Sastra Adharalu* (Foundations of Educational Psychology). Guntur: Sri Nagarjuna Publishers.

Lalini, V., V. Dayakara Reddy, M. Srihari and Digumarti Bhaskara Rao, (2004). *Vidya Adharalu* (Foundations of Education). Guntur: Sri Nagarjuna Publishers.

Subba Rao, K.P., P. Ayodhya and Digumarti Bhaskara Rao, (2004). *Patasala Yajamanyam—Vidhya Vyavasthalu* (School Management and Systems of Education). Guntur: Sri Nagarjuna Publishers.

Sudhakar, V., B. Ravindra Babu, D.S. Kumar and Digumarti Bhaskara Rao, (2004). *Vidya Sanketika Sastram—Computer Vidhya* (Educational Technology and Computer Education). Guntur: Sri Nagarjuna Publishers.

INDEX

V

W

□□□